WHICH FISH IS THAT?

EXPLORE AUSTRALIA

ACKNOWLEDGEMENTS
General Editor Steve Cooper
Fisheries Consultant Ross Winstanley
Design and page layout Adrian Saunders
Project Manager Astrid Browne
Editorial Assistance Rachel Pitts, Emma Schwarcz
Index Fay Donlevy

Explore Australia Publishing Pty Ltd
85 High Street
Prahran, Victoria 3181, Australia

First edition published by Explore Australia Publishing Pty Ltd, 2003

10 9 8 7 6 5 4 3

Much of the material in this book originally appeared in
Fish Australia, published by Penguin Books, 2002. The information has
been updated for this new publication.

Printed and bound in China by Toppan Leefung Printing Limited

National Library of Australia
Cataloguing-in-Publication data

Includes index.
ISBN 13 978 1 74117 012 2

1. Fishing – Australia. 2. Fishes – Australia – Identification.

799.10994

Publisher's note
Every effort has been made to ensure that the information in this book is
accurate at the time of going to press. The publisher welcomes information
and suggestions for correction or improvement. Write to the Publications
Manager, Explore Australia Publishing, 85 High Street, Prahran, Victoria
3181, Australia or email explore@hardiegrant.com.au

Illustrations
Illustrations are by Roger Swainston/Anima and Walter Stackpool
(reproduced with permission from Jack Pollard, *The Complete Illustrated
Guide to Fish*, Transworld, Sydney, 1991).

Cover illustrations: red emperor/Roger Swainston/Anima; rainbow trout
and Australian bass/Walter Stackpool (copyright owned by Jack Pollard).

Photographs by Bill Bachman, Ross Barnett, Richard I'Anson,
Trevor Percival, photolibrary.com, Retrospect (Dale Mann),
Warren Steptoe, Stock Photos (Robert Gray, Bruce Peebles), Peter Walton.

Contents

HOW TO FISH

FISH IDENTIFICATION

FISHNET
.COM.AU

Australia's largest fishing magazine and fishing club

Visit Fishnet for your latest weather & fishing reports

Estuary and Bay Fishing

Half of Australia's estimated four million anglers fish in estuaries and bays, because they offer easy access to a variety of fish in safety and comfort and a range of locations and habitats.

Estuary and bay anglers fish from land and structures such as piers, or from boats. Estuaries exist in bays and inlets, wherever fresh water meets salt. Many fish spend their entire lives in the estuary, but it is also a spawning ground, nursery and feeding area for fish from the open ocean.

When to fish

Most fish inhabiting estuaries and bays feed at dawn and dusk; their behaviour is strongly influenced by tides. For the angler, forward planning is important and should include: deciding on the species you are trying to catch, collecting bait, preparing berley, setting suitable tackle and considering the effect that tide and time of day will have on where you fish.

Dawn and dusk feeders, such as bream, flathead, whiting, snapper and mulloway, will feed in the shallows in low light but seek safer depths during the day. Mullet, leatherjacket and luderick are less demanding about time of day, but their behaviour is influenced by the tides.

In temperate climes snapper, hairtail, luderick, mullet and bream move in and out of bays and estuaries according to season and locality. Generally, fishing is best during the warmer months, from September through to April. During winter many estuary dwellers move to deeper offshore waters, returning in spring to spawn. In the tropics, species like barramundi, trevally, threadfin salmon and mangrove jack also move according to season and locality. The seasons in this region are predominantly the Wet and the Dry. During the Wet, which starts around November and lasts through to March or April, there are fish to be caught, but the Dry season is more conducive to fishing the northern estuaries.

Where to fish

Fish within estuaries and bays tend to base their lives around structures – whether artificial, like wharves and bridges, or natural ones, like weed beds and holes.

Sand or mudflats that are exposed at low tide are excellent areas to explore when the tide is rising. In southern estuaries, whiting, bream and flathead will search for food there, and trevally, shark and even barramundi will hunt through the shallows feeding on bait fish. The best fishing occurs on flats that have a deep channel or gutter running alongside. A good flat will have around 1 m or more of water over it at high tide.

In many bays and estuaries, you can fish quite effectively from shoreline features such as river banks or from structures such as piers or breakwalls. In the mangrove-lined estuaries of the far north, a boat is almost essential.

Piers are more common in bays and lakes, but are also found in some rivers. In many estuarine rivers, breakwalls provide deepwater access for land-based angling. Bridges are often good spots as well, provided that fishing is allowed from them.

Wherever you fish from the shore, choose places where the fish have some reason to gather or pass by.

A boat is usually necessary to fish Australia's northern estuaries

It helps if you incorporate some form of berleying to attract them.

The keys to successful land-based fishing are to be prepared, have the right tackle and bait for the species you are after, and work the tides so you are there at the same time as the fish.

Bait

Locally available baits are the best choice. A type of burrowing shrimp found in southern estuaries, variously called 'yabby', 'bass yabby' or 'pink nipper', lives in tidal sand flats and can be gathered with a suction pump. Similar 'green nippers' found in more northern regions can be 'puddled' by treading shallow weed beds and scooping them from the surface. They can also be found under rocks and logs exposed by a falling tide. Bloodworms and squirt worms can be dug or pumped, using a bait pump, from exposed tidal flats. Prawns, shrimp, small fish and squid are good baits, as are cockles, oysters and mussels.

Other useful baits include the various whitebait, pilchard and bluebait. They are best for flathead, though large flathead prefer tiny live mullet. Baits of fresh striped tuna and squid are also effective and chicken gut is popular for bream in Queensland.

You do not need bait for all species. Many will attack lures, and tackle shops can often advise which lures work best on the fish in their locality.

Target fish

The six most common estuary species are bream, flathead, mullet, mulloway, snapper and whiting. Others, such as barramundi, estuary perch, flounder, garfish, hairtail, mangrove jack, tailor and trevally, are important on a regional or seasonal basis.

Bream prefer areas offering a structure and shelter. The three main species are black bream, yellowfin bream and pikey bream. Unlike most other estuarine species, bream stay in the estuary over winter.

Tuna and kingfish are the target at the Merimbula Wharf

Flathead come in more than a dozen forms, but three commonly encountered species are sand flathead, dusky flathead and yank flathead. In estuaries flathead favour the edges of sandbanks, scattered patches of weed and any place where the current is deflected into eddies.

Mullet are one of the most widespread families of fish in Australia. Common types include: sea, fantail (silver), yelloweye, flat-tail, tiger, diamond-scale, pop-eye and sand (lano, tallegalane). Of these, the most easily line-caught types are the sand, yelloweye and tiger mullets.

Mulloway (jewfish) frequent areas around bridges, points, holes and creek mouths, where they hunt or ambush their favoured foods of small fish, prawns or squid. Live or dead baits of these are effective, as are large minnow-style lures.

Juvenile **snapper** live in temperate bays and estuaries along the east coast of New South Wales and Queensland. Periodically, big fish move into sheltered waters, usually in spring and summer. In summer, numbers of large adults are also found in Port Phillip and Western Port, in Victoria, and Gulf St Vincent and Spencer Gulf, in South Australia.

There are some eight common species of **whiting**; of these the best known are the trumpeter and sand whiting of the eastern seaboard, the yellow-finned whiting of Western Australia and South Australia, and the King George whiting, plentiful in South Australia and Victoria but less abundant in New South Wales, Tasmania and Western Australia. Whiting leave estuaries in winter.

Barramundi and **mangrove jack** often co-exist in mangrove-lined tidal creeks, frequenting the intersections of main and feeder streams. You can also find them around rocky points on bays and inshore islands.

Garfish are a common catch in estuaries and bays. They can be berleyed up with bread or pollard and caught on tiny baits of uncooked prawn, fish flesh or bread dough.

Leatherjacket are delicious to eat and easy to catch in good numbers once you have found their hiding places. These include deep water underneath jetties and alongside weed beds. Bait up with small baits on long-shank hooks and periodically toss in berley.

Luderick mainly inhabit the east coast of New South Wales, Victoria and northern Tasmania. The adult fish are residents of the wash areas fronting ocean rocks. Luderick also spend much of their lives inside estuaries, bays and coastal lakes. They take baits of green weed, sea-lettuce, squirt worms and pink nippers, and are usually best fished with a long flexible rod, light line and a float.

Tailor are common through New South Wales and southern Queensland, in good numbers from the south to mid-coast of Western Australia. Most estuary tailor, known as 'choppers', weigh up to 1 kg and will readily take either baits or lures.

Trevally frequent many estuaries, the silver variety being common in temperate zones, with species such as giant, golden, gold-spotted and bigeye usually found further north. Most trevally will take lures; all will take baits of small fish. Silvers will also take various worms, crustaceans and shellfish.

In the tropical north, estuaries can yield **pikey bream**, **barramundi**, **threadfin salmon**, **mangrove jack**, several types of **trevally**, **black jewfish (mulloway)**, **estuary cod** and **fingermark**. The nature of tropical estuaries and creeks is such that you may find them easier to fish on the smaller neap tides than the much larger spring tides.

Rock and
Beach Fishing

**Land-based saltwater fishing can range from
a gentle beach activity to the challenge of
ocean-ravaged rocks and cliffs.**

Rocky ledges and headlands all along the coast are
interspersed with long stretches of beach, often away
from population centres.

Most capital cities in Australia are within easy
reach of ocean beaches, readily accessed by two-wheel
drive vehicles. Visiting anglers can have a rod in the
water within an hour or two of leaving home.

For the more intrepid angler there are beaches in
remote parts of the country, particularly in the west,
north and north-east of Australia. A four-wheel drive

Fishing from breakwalls is effective

will often be required to reach these places that are 'off the beaten track'.

Rock fishing should always be approached with care. Some of the rocky platforms that front deep ocean water demand anglers exercise good sense and caution. When fishing from rocks at sea level, most of the threat comes from the water itself. Large waves can mount the rocks and wash the unwary in, and natural growths of weed and algae can make surfaces slippery underfoot.

The dangers of high-cliff fishing are obvious. There are also hidden traps, such as sandstone ledges that can be worn treacherously thin by erosion and weakened by saltwater absorption.

When to fish

When fishing this 'edge of Australia', the tides come into play in a marked way. Low water can virtually obliterate holes and gutters on a beach, sending fish out to deeper water. On the rocks, low tide can create a stretch of broken rock between you and the water

Time, tide, weather and terrain affect the success and safety of the rock angler

into which you want to cast. High tides can improve the fishing opportunities or wipe them out – it all depends on the terrain and the weather.

By intelligently using tide charts and some knowledge of local terrain, you can prepare fishing plans that use the tides to best effect, and place you within safe and comfortable casting distance of fish that have been moved about by the changing water levels. An understanding of the feeding habits of your target species can help you focus your efforts on those times and places when the fish are likely to be in the greatest numbers.

The fishing from beach and rocks along the east coast of Australia is best from November to May. This period coincides with the warmer Pacific currents moving closer to shore, bringing with them the bait fish and the larger fish that chase the bait schools. The further north you go the more extensive the fishing season becomes. The Great Barrier Reef protects the inshore waters and fish are present and active all year round.

The west coast is exposed to the big Indian Ocean swells. Here, pelagics such as mackerel, tuna and shark can be taken all year round.

South from Perth, across the Bight to South Australia and into Victoria, rock fishing is not as good, but there is excellent surf fishing in the cooler months for such species as tailor, Australian salmon, mulloway and gummy shark.

Rock fishing

Holes and gutters and inshore reefs, which break the force of the surging water, attract and hold fish around the rocks. Small fish, including yellowtail, garfish and sweep, tend to school quite close to the rocks, but usually at some depth. Larger foraging species, such as bream, blackfish, drummer and groper, skirt the rock face and work in close under the line of white water. More active fish, like snapper, yellowtail kingfish, tailor and Australian salmon, roam a little further out, calling in to the shoreline to make feeding raids or to get away from larger predators. The big surface fish of the summer months, such as longtail and yellowfin tuna, shark and even marlin, will also move in close to the rocks in season. Mulloway (jewfish), on the other hand, tend to keep close to particular reefs, caves and gutters, usually venturing out on hunting sprees at first or last light, or when it is dark.

Basically there are two types of rock fishing practised around Australia. The first could be called baitfishing for species for the table. In southern Australia, these species include parrotfish, sweep and pike, and further north along the New South Wales coast, luderick, rock blackfish, drummer, groper and even snapper are the more common catches.

The other method of rock fishing practised is often referred to as land-based game fishing, and ranges from high-speed spinning for tuna to various live-bait fishing techniques for species such as tuna, yellowtail kingfish, mackerel, giant trevally and even marlin.

Your tackle should be appropriate for the fish and the conditions. It is helpful if rods are around 3 m or more. Your line should be a little heavier than that used in sheltered waters, both to withstand the punishment of the terrain and also to control the fish, which will often be larger than those found in estuaries.

There will be times when your rod and line will not be strong enough to land some fish and, in these instances, a gaff on a suitably long pole is a practical fishing tool. Anglers fishing from high cliffs are faced

Watch the water when rock fishing at sea level

with unique problems in landing fish, and they may need to use a grapnel or flying gaff to secure their played-out fish and hoist it up.

Beach fishing

In the same way that fish are attracted to depth and to rock areas, and feed most freely around such features, they are at least partly predictable in their use of various seabed structures when they visit ocean beaches.

Even so, the operative fish-attracting features of beaches are anything but permanent, often changing from week to week.

On any given day, it is likely you will have to check the beach before fishing it to see what changes have occurred. In periods of stable weather, formations may persist for a long time. On more exposed beaches, the changes can be sudden and dramatic.

Australia's classic deep beaches extend from Fraser Island on the east coast, south to Victoria, across the Bight then north along the coast of Western Australia to Shark Bay. North of Fraser Island and Shark Bay, the beaches become much shallower.

Beaches are like highways and feeding places through which the fish pass. In the tide line areas there is an abundance of marine life. There may be channels, gutters, drop-offs and banks close inshore as well as further out. The tide line and close-in areas are the likely spots for foraging fish such as whiting, luderick and bream, while gutters and holes are popular places of concealment for predators such as mulloway, salmon, tailor and flathead.

Gutters inside offshore sandbanks are excellent for whiting and bream, as the wave action over the

Tailor is one of the main targets for beach anglers

bank dislodges amounts of sand and the food within it to the foraging fish.

Tailor, bream, flathead and salmon are common beach fish and tend to inhabit the midline between the inshore waters and the outer gutters. Mulloway favour the deeper channels and holes.

Beach fishing tackle, suitable for tailor, Australian salmon, bream and whiting, usually consists of a 3 to 3.5-m rod, and a reel of your choice spooled with 4 to 8-kg line. If targeting larger fish, such as mulloway or gummy shark, you may need heavier tackle or at least a trace of heavier line for insurance.

Bait

In many cases, the best baits available will be lying buried beneath the sand you are standing on – beachworms, sand crabs, or shellfish known in various locales as pippis, eugaries or cockles. Other beach baits include pilchards, whitebait and bluebait, and strip baits of fish, squid and mussels.

Often, if you arrive at low tide or at the last of the run-out, you can gather your bait from the beach before you start to fish. At this time, the intertidal area inhabited by these sand dwellers is freshly exposed and they are still close to the surface.

Target fish

Around the southern perimeter of Australia, beach species include bream, whiting, flathead, tailor, Australian salmon and mulloway. From the rocks you can add groper, drummer, rock blackfish, luderick, snapper, yellowtail kingfish and mackerel, and occasional visitors such as trevally, sweetlip, cobia, sailfish, marlin and yellowfin tuna, as well as various other surface speedsters such as bonito and striped and mackerel tuna.

Offshore Fishing

There are many options for the offshore angler: fishing around reefs and rocks or over gravel beds, sand or mud, fishing the bottom with a heavy sinker and hooks on droppers, fishing with unweighted baits, drifting, trolling, or fishing from an anchored position.

Broadly speaking, offshore fishing in Australia encompasses trolling for game and sport fish, bottom fishing with bait, jigging lures for reef-dwelling species, or lure casting for sport fish around structures such as bomboras, reefs and washes.

Most offshore fishing is done in proximity to land – near reefs and islands or near the mainland shore itself. However, there is also good fishing to be had in more open water where the ocean currents play the major role in attracting pelagic fish.

Reading the water

Inshore, around shallow reefs, headlands and islands, it is easy to recognise areas where fish might be gathered, but out in open water it is different. Fish will be spread over a wide area and their whereabouts must be gauged by guesswork and intuition.

The colour of the water indicates temperature changes: warm water appears to be bluish and colder water has a greener tinge.

Many species of fish prefer to feed under the cover of darkness, or at least at half light. Some fish that would not go anywhere near shallow water during the day can be attracted by the half light of dawn or dusk, or the darkness of night, to move into water barely deep enough to cover them. Others, like tuna and marlin, seem not to be affected by light.

The roughness of the sea also affects general fish behaviour. A moderate degree of wind and wave action is beneficial to fishing, as the associated white water and wind chop allows fish to move about with reduced risk from predators.

Turbulence can stimulate feeding, as there is often more to eat at such times. Wave action tears food loose from reefs and rock ledges. Prey species are driven by currents and wind into concentrations, providing an easily harvested food supply.

Fish that have a high metabolic rate feed almost constantly, and have a correspondingly high level of oxygen demand. Many surface-feeding species must roam extensively to find food; they burn up vast amounts of oxygen just to survive. Such species include mackerel, marlin and tuna.

More sedentary species, such as snapper, bream or mulloway, have slower metabolic rates and less

Offshore fishing gives anglers great access to larger deepwater species

continuous periods of activity. They often browse, rest or drift with the moving water, generally close to cover and always where they are most comfortable.

Game fishing

Game fishing is a popular pastime and thirty years ago, most game fishing in Australia was conducted from large professional charter boats. Nowadays there is an even larger charter-boat industry in addition to thousands of anglers who fish offshore in private craft from around 4 to 20 m in length.

Large game fish are likely to be where there are warm, blue, ocean currents pushing southwards from the tropics. Other indicators are surface-feeding schools of intermediate predators, such as striped tuna or frigate mackerel. In turn, big fish such as yellowfin tuna, marlin or shark move in to feed.

Feeding pods of fish are often signposted by wheeling flocks of sea birds, but you can also stumble across them by trolling along current lines. Generally, the more current lines and the warmer and bluer the water, the better.

Game fishing methods include trolling lures, trolling dead 'skip' baits, trolling live baits, fishing live or dead baits from a drifting boat and at times (although rarely) fishing baits from an anchored boat.

Reef fishing

Not everyone who fishes offshore, however, will set their sights on game fish, nor do they need to. Fish, such as emperor, snapper, yellowtail kingfish, cobia, mackerel, tailor and mulloway, inhabit inshore reefs, headland and island areas, and can be pursued with smaller boats and less sophisticated tackle.

When fishing offshore reefs for a variety of species on the bottom, there is often an opportunity to pursue

Game fishing often requires the use of a harness and heavy tackle

many sport fish that come past. Small mackerel tuna, snook, queenfish, trevally and barracouta are some of the sport fish found around offshore reefs.

Using berley offshore

Berley is used in all forms of offshore fishing, including game and sportfishing as well as fishing over a reef for bottom dwellers. Sending down a cloud of easily-gathered food among a bunch of sleepy fish can change their attitude dramatically.

Offshore berley can be made from pieces of fish flesh and various fish oils, either used alone or mixed together and extended with some kind of cereal product, such as bread or stock-food pellets. It can be dispensed in various ways: through a berley bucket or berley bomb, or simply tossed over the side.

The key with berley is to use the right type and just enough to get the job done. A little, in a constant stream, is better than a big slug of it, then nothing. This is especially important offshore, where currents can take the berley away from you, and the fish with it. Remember, do not feed the fish! Berley should only stimulate them.

Locating the catch

Regardless of the style of offshore fishing you pursue, it is important to fish in the right place, where all the hungry fish are congregated.

A depth sounder can be a big advantage offshore. Good sounders can pinpoint offshore reefs in 20 m of water and often locate fish over that structure as well.

Having found your fish, all that is required is to determine the best rig and approach. You do not need a rod and rig for every fish in the ocean, but you do need to take into account that fish differ in size, aggression and eating habits. You should have a range of tackle on board and be adequately prepared.

At the simple end of things, you could get away with a set of light and heavy handlines, but by rod fishing you give yourself added versatility, being able to cast, troll, drift or bottom fish with a variety of baits or lures.

Saltwater fly casting for tuna in the Gulf of Carpentaria

Inland Fishing

Fly fishing is just one of the wide variety of freshwater fishing experiences available in Australia, each with its own excitement, fascination and keen devotees.

While much of the Australian inland is very dry and virtually devoid of permanent waterways, the greater part of the coastal fringe enjoys good rainfall, and a resultant abundance of rivers and lakes.

Most inland waters remain public property and Australian anglers generally enjoy a right of access to rivers and lakes.

From the premier trout fisheries of Tasmania to the barramundi stocks of northern Australia, there is something for every angling taste.

Baitfishing

Baitfishing is the simplest and most widely known form of freshwater fishing. Nowadays, baitfishing can be quite complex. For example, bait drifting – the casting and retrieving of virtually unweighted baits – requires perfectly tuned equipment and a good knowledge of natural baits.

Another form of baitfishing called coarse angling has developed into a distinct sport on its own. Coarse angling uses berley extensively: quantities of bread crumbs and similar mixtures to lure fish into the area the angler is fishing. It is now very popular in Australia, where the techniques work on a wide range of species – including trout. Many coarse anglers employ highly specialised equipment such as long and very sensitive rods and finely tuned floats, and choose from an array of surprisingly small hooks. Baits are

Baitfishing for species such as Murray cod and golden perch in the Condamine River, Queensland

also quite different to those normally used by regular bait fishers, and include maggots (gents), corn kernels and dough.

Despite the complexities of bait drifting and coarse angling, basic baitfishing remains a great technique for the casual angler, beginners and children. There is a delightful simplicity in a rod and threadline reel. Rigged with 3-kg line and either a small sinker or a float about half to one metre above a hook baited with a common bait like worms or shrimp, it remains an easy and effective method for catching many species. Redfin, eel, golden and silver perch, river blackfish, catfish, trout and sooty grunter are some fish that can be caught by basic baitfishing.

Successful anglers have learned that using light gear and carefully approaching the water helps success.

Lure casting and trolling lures

Lure casting involves casting and retrieving lures that either mimic bait fish and other fish food, or simply 'trigger' an attack response in fish. Trolling works on the same principle. Lure casting and trolling work best on active predators including barramundi, sooty grunter, redfin, golden perch, Australian bass, trout and Murray cod.

There are now endless varieties of lures on the market, including models that dive to great depth or wriggle along the surface. There are also spinners that have a flashing revolving blade, and even lures that contain a rattle to attract fish.

Lure fishing can be as simple as trolling a wobbler behind a moving boat, or as complex as casting just the right lure to just the right location, and retrieving it at just the right speed and depth. Experienced anglers target a particular fish species, and use gear that is not unnecessarily heavy.

Fly fishing

Fly fishing is the art of casting almost weightless artificial lures called flies, which are made from materials such as fur and feather or modern substitutes. Because these flies have so little weight, conventional casting does not work. Instead, fly fishers use comparatively heavy lines and long flexible rods. The fly line is cast back and forth in the air until sufficient line speed is built up to enable the fly to be presented to the desired target.

The fly line is too thick to attach a hook, so a leader (a length of tapered fishing line) is linked to the end of the fly line, and to this is tied the fly itself. It takes practice to learn the timing and technique required to keep the fly line airborne and then deliver the final cast and present the fly. A few days of informed practice is usually enough to cast well enough to begin catching fish.

While trout are still the number one target of fly fishers, more anglers are discovering that nearly every fish that swims can be caught on the fly. Fly fishing for trout will always remain especially popular because trout respond so well to the technique. Trout frequently feed on small insects like mayflies or caddis that may be only fingernail size, floating on the surface. When 'rising' to such tiny, buoyant insects, trout are all but uncatchable to anyone but fly fishers using dry (floating) artificial flies.

Wet (sinking) flies can be used for trout and many other species. The huge diversity of wet fly patterns available means that just about every form of aquatic life is realistically copied. Unlike dry flies, which are usually left to drift naturally on lake or stream, wet flies are normally retrieved to impart a swimming motion that matches that of the organism being imitated.

Whether using wet or dry flies, fly fishers sometimes utilise an interesting technique called polaroiding. Polarised sunglasses remove much of the glare and reflection from the water surface, enabling much clearer vision beneath it. If light conditions and water clarity are favourable, fly fishers wearing polaroids can locate their target fish, and present their fly to the right spot.

South-eastern Australia

New South Wales, Victoria and Tasmania have abundant freshwater fishing on offer. The Great Dividing Range, which arcs south then west through New South Wales and Victoria, is the source of every significant river in these two States. It is in and around these hills and mountains, in cool, clean water, that

Fly fishing is the art of casting almost weightless artificial lures called flies

the trout, the most sought-after freshwater sport fish, is found. In Victoria, trout thrive in many waters at or near sea level, and a long way from true mountain country. Across Bass Strait, Tasmania has the cream of Australian trout fishing. This large island has proved an ideal habitat for trout, and most freshwater lakes and streams (and many estuaries) hold good numbers.

In all three States, trout are the only significant angling species in the true alpine country, but as the elevation decreases, trout begin to share their habitat with other angling species. Redfin co-exist with trout in many lakes and rivers, and extend beyond this range to inhabit many of the slower, warmer waters of the inland. Also caught from immediately outside the alpine country through to the edge of the warm inland waters are two sought-after native fish: Macquarie perch and river blackfish. Macquarie perch is the rarer of the two, and does best in Victoria.

Three superb warm-water natives, Murray cod, golden perch and silver perch, are making a strong comeback in many inland waters in Victoria and New

South Wales, particularly those that flow west into the Murray–Darling system. They are also making a comeback into several impoundments that previously held only trout and redfin. Lakes such as Burrinjuck, Hume and Eildon now offer a blend of cool and warm-water species.

The coastal streams of New South Wales contain another top native sport fish, the Australian bass. As one moves into coastal Victoria, these fish are replaced by a less well-known relative, the estuary perch. Bass, in particular, have returned to sport fishing prominence in recent years, thanks to large-scale hatchery breeding and the stocking of artificial lakes.

Of the four south-eastern States, South Australia is the poorest for freshwater fishing, simply because so much of it is desert country devoid of permanent lakes and rivers. However, the Murray River does offer fishing for golden perch, silver perch, Murray cod and redfin, and smaller streams around Adelaide contain some trout.

As well as the species already mentioned, anglers in south-eastern freshwater areas may also encounter eel and tench, and that most destructive invader, the European carp. Any carp caught should be killed immediately.

Western Australia

Australia's largest State provides an enormous variety of freshwater fishing commensurate with its range of freshwater environments. The south-western corner has a temperate climate similar to Victoria and southern New South Wales. Not surprisingly, this area is the home of the west's trout fishery.

Redfin are very successful in the south-west, and frequently overlap with trout. Native angling species of significance are rare in the area, although the locals enjoy catching a delicious crustacean called marron.

From just north of Perth through to the start of the Kimberley, freshwater fishing is limited.

There is an abrupt change for the better once the remote tropics of the Kimberley are reached. Heavy monsoonal rains over summer feed a number of major rivers, and many permanent and semi-permanent lagoons. These waters are home to numerous tropical species, the most famous of which is the barramundi. As well as barramundi, freshwater anglers may encounter species as diverse as long tom, giant catfish and various species of perch.

Northern Australia

The Top End of the Northern Territory, Queensland's Cape York Peninsula, and the Gulf Country that separates the two, provide a continuation of the excellent tropical freshwater fishing found in the

Normanby River, Cape York: Northern Australia is renowned for its diversity of freshwater species

Kimberley. Barramundi continues to be the most prized sport fish, with species like sooty grunter and saratoga also popular.

Moving south from Cape York Peninsula, Queensland freshwater fishing changes. Ambitious stocking programs for impoundments have improved freshwater fishing significantly. Lake Tinaroo on the Atherton Tableland is producing big barramundi as well as sooty grunter. Further south, stocking with other species like golden perch, bass and saratoga is proving successful.

The Darling River feeder streams west of the Great Divide provide native fish like those found further down the system, with golden perch especially abundant. Catfish are found in eastern-flowing streams, with jungle perch in some tropical mountain streams in the north, and Mary River cod in the Maryborough area. South of the Noosa River, Australian bass can be caught in the coastal rivers where the habitat is suitable.

The Inland

Beyond the coastal rivers and the Murray–Darling system lies the dry inner core of Australia, containing rare small pockets of water inhabited by tiny, hardy fish that have no angling appeal.

Saltwater Fish

Albacore
Thunnus alalunga

Also known as longfin tuna.

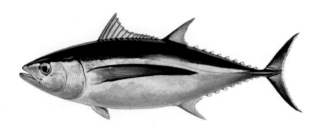

Location/Description

Found in offshore waters and usually in schools, the albacore is recognised by its exceptionally long pectoral fins, which extend well beyond the second dorsal. Although it can grow to 40 kg, it is commonly captured at 2 to 5 kg. The fish is irridescent blue along the top with a silvery belly. It is prized for its fight, particularly when encountered in a large school. Its table quality is also excellent, the meat being almost white when cooked, whereas the meat of other tunas is mostly red and oily.

Fishing method

This fish is mostly caught by trolling or jigging with lures, live baiting with yellowtail or slimy mackerel, or drift fishing with berley and bait of cubed fish flesh. It inhabits the warm ocean currents in waters well offshore.

Amberjack
Seriola dumerili

Location/Description

A close tropical relative of the yellowtail kingfish, the amberjack is a large powerful pelagic fish and reaches 2 m in length and 80 kg in weight. It forms large schools, usually deeper than 20 m, and is often caught around reefs by anglers and commercial fishermen trolling for mackerel or fishing for snapper and other reef fish. Although it presents a challenge for anglers, it lacks the eating qualities of some of its close relatives. Smaller amberjack make the best eating and should be bled immediately.

Fishing method

Fish over heavy reef and structure in deep water. Shows a preference for live baits but can be difficult to get strip baits down to. Amberjack will also take lures but these have to be run deep for the best results. When choosing an outfit err on the heavy side and use 6/0 to 8/0 hooks for live bait.

Barracouta
Thyrsites atun

Also known as axehandle, couta, pickhandle.

Location/Description

The barracouta is a pelagic, schooling, cold-water fish. When caught in warmer waters it is rarely good eating because of parasitic worms and 'milky' flesh, but it is a regularly sold commercial species in Australia's south. This long, slender fish is fast and voracious but even a 1.5 m specimen will not weigh much more than 5 or 6 kg. It is blue-black on top, fading down the sides to a silvery belly. The black dorsal fin is long and low, and the protruding jaws are lined with large, needle-sharp teeth.

Fishing method

Barracouta will bite anything (a piece of red or white rag, even a bare shiny hook), but is usually fished by trolling or casting with whitebait, bacon rind, fish strips, or a variety of lures. A wire trace is necessary because of its teeth.

Barracuda
Sphyraena barracuda

Also known as cuda, dingo fish.

Location/Description

The barracuda inhabits tropical estuaries and creeks as juveniles, and beaches and reefs as adults. It has a generally silver body, sometimes with brown bands and with distinct spots toward the tail. Its teeth are large and dagger-like, and it can attain 1.7 m and up to 25 kg. Handling a well-toothed fish of this size requires care and common sense. No kitchen prizes here, particularly as the bigger fish are known to be linked with cases of ciguatera poisoning (when caught off the east coast). Even the small fish are best returned and not eaten.

Fishing method

This fish is mostly caught incidentally, because its food value is low and its fight, while brutal, is of only short duration. A wire trace can save lures too expensive to lose, while heavy mono will suffice for bait fishing when the only loss is likely to be a hook and sinker.

Barramundi

Lates calcarifer

Also known as barra, giant perch.

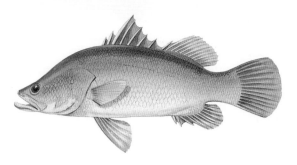

Location/Description

One of Australia's favourite fish, the barramundi is a respected angling opponent and good eating. Reportedly reaching 1.5 m and 50 kg, the majority caught weigh less than 6 kg. It travels from fresh to salt water to spawn and, while in salt water, is silvery and bronze. Landlocked fish are generally darker, they don't fight as well, and their table quality is inferior. Almost all barramundi less than 5 years of age are male and some become female at a certain size, so large fish are vitally important brood stock.

Fishing method

Barramundi respond best to live bait or lures, but will also take well-presented strip baits. Line sizes from 4 to 10 kg are appropriate and boat fishing, either trolling or casting, is the most favoured method.

Blackfish, rock

Girella elevata

Also known as black drummer, blackfish, pig.

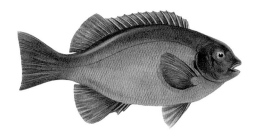

Location/Description

The rock blackfish grows to around 8 kg, but the most common catch ranges from 1 to 2 kg. It is a dark, rotund, small-mouthed herbivorous species with the occasional urge to eat meat, and with the ability to romp happily in rocky water rough enough to smash lesser fish to a pulp. It is found all along the east coast of Australia from Noosa Heads in Queensland to Victoria, but not in western Victoria or South Australia. Its western relative, G. *tephraeops*, is found on coastal reefs of south-western Western Australia.

Fishing method

Serious rock blackfish anglers use stout rods, sidecast reels and line from 10 to 20 kg. Bobby corks help to minimise tackle losses, and hooks should be double or triple X strong in sizes from No. 1 to 2/0.

Bonefish

Albula vulpes

Also known as ladyfish.

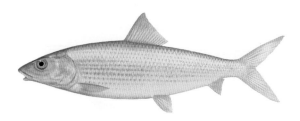

Location/Description

Occurring in inshore habitats in northern Australia, the bonefish is superficially quite similar to a whiting. However, it is readily distinguished by its single dorsal fin (whiting have two) and its small under-slung mouth. It reaches larger sizes (up to 90 cm and 5 kg) and lacks the fine eating qualities common to most whiting. Unfortunately, while the bonefish provides excellent angling and is highly rated as a game fish, it is not frequently caught by anglers.

Fishing method

Bonefish is the unicorn fish of Australia's inshore sand flats for saltwater fly fishers. A most sought after yet rarely encountered species, most bonefish caught in our waters have been caught by accident on bait in deep water. Fish strips worked in a berley trail while drifting seems to be the successful method.

Bonito
Sarda australis

Also known as bonnie, horse mackerel, horsie.

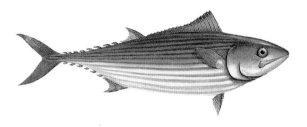

Location/Description

Found in coastal waters of New South Wales, southern Queensland and southern Western Australia, this member of the tuna family has horizontal dark stripes on its back and sides, differing from the similar oriental bonito (*S. orientalis*), a west coast species, striped only on its upper half. Another species, Watson's leaping bonito (*Cybiosarda elegans*), is found in east coast waters and is characterised by a high dorsal fin, belly stripes and broken wavy markings from shoulder to tail on its back.

Fishing method

Strip baits or small live fish can be used, but bonito is best caught by trolling or casting with lures: usually small chromed metal slices, swimming minnows or saltwater flies. Top time is dawn. Bonito frequent wash areas of rocky headlands and inshore islands.

Bream, black

Acanthopagrus butcheri

Also known as southern black bream, southern bream.

Location/Description

Black bream is the most commonly found member of this family in southern waters. It favours estuaries and inshore waters where it feeds on various marine worms, crustacea, shellfish, juvenile molluscs and fin-fish. Anglers can expect to catch a few good-sized examples of this fine table fish in any southern estuary. Its body colour varies between dull gold and silvery olive-brown. Similar in colouration but of different body shape, the pikey bream is found only in the tropics.

Fishing method

Light lines from 2 to 6 kg, depending on terrain, and baits of worms, nippers or even tuna strips are best. Black bream (and pikey bream) will also attack small lures if they are accurately cast and worked close to structures where these fish lie in wait.

Bream, pikey

Acanthopagrus berda

Also known as black bream.

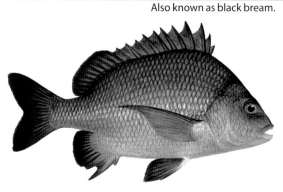

Location/Description

This is the common bream of northern Queensland, where it occurs in fresh, brackish, and marine waters, particularly in muddy coastal habitats near creeks, piers, and mangroves. While it grows up to 56 cm, most of those caught are around 35 cm. It is readily caught by fishing close to structures where larger fish present anglers with an exciting challenge to catch them before they become snagged or break off. Like other bream species, it is an excellent eating fish having firm, white, flaky flesh.

Fishing method

Pikey bream can be found around wharves, jetties, and estuaries. This fish likes to hang on structure. Popular method is to fish a prawn or sandworm on a running sinker rig with hooks from about No. 4 to 1/0. Pikey bream can also be caught on small soft plastic and minnow style lures and salt water flies worked-in close to cover.

Bream, yellowfin
Acanthopagrus australis

Also known as eastern black bream, sea bream, silver bream, surf bream.

Location/Description

Yellowfin bream has a much narrower geographical range than black bream. This handsome silver fish has bright to dull yellow pelvic and anal fins. The head is more sharply pointed than the black bream and the clear to yellowish tail has a distinct black trailing edge. It inhabits surf beaches as well as estuaries in northern and central New South Wales, and Queensland. In common with other members of the bream family, it becomes extremely cunning as it matures. It is a popular table fish.

Fishing method

Popular baits include live nippers, live or dead crabs, prawns, shrimp, live marine worms, strip baits of fish flesh, squid or octopus, or whole pippis or other shellfish. Yellowfin bream will also take small lures.

Catfish, fork-tailed

Arius leptaspis

Also known as croaker, salmon catfish.

Location/Description

Fork-tailed catfish are collectively referred to as salmon catfish, and the different species include: the one illustrated here, *Arius leptaspis*, the blue (*A. graffei*), the threadfin (*A. armiger*), the lesser salmon catfish (*A. berneyi*) and the small-mouthed salmon catfish (*Cinetodus froggatti*). They are all freshwater, estuarine or marine fish and inhabit tropical waters. The fork-tailed catfish can change its body colour to suit its environment. The males of some species hold the eggs in their mouths.

Fishing method

Essentially a bottom feeder, this species will take most fish flesh baits and can also be taken on lures. It will often take lures intended for other fish, such as barramundi. Line from 4 to 6 kg and a medium weight baitcaster or threadline outfit is ideal.

Cobbler

Cnidoglanis macrocephalus

Also known as catfish, estuary catfish.

Location/Description

The cobbler is one of the most highly valued angling species in Western Australia because of its soft sweet-tasting flesh. It occurs most frequently on sandy and weedy bottom in the estuaries of the south-west coast. Cobbler stocks have declined because of fishing pressure (including previously allowed netting and trapping), with many being taken before they reach sexual maturity. Anglers should take particular care to avoid the three venomous spines on the dorsal and pectoral fins.

Fishing method

Prawns and worms fished on the bottom do well on cobblers. These baits should be used in conjunction with a light running sinker rig for best results. Cobblers lurk about estuarine weed, both growing and washed-up.

Cobia

Rachycentron canadus

Also known as black king, black kingfish, cobe, crab-eater, ling, sergeant fish.

Location/Description

The cobia is a handsome game fish found in oceanic waters from temperate to sub-tropical climes. It frequents areas around navigation beacons, deepwater wharves, headlands, offshore islands and over reefs. It is blackish-brown with a creamy stripe along its sides, and its streamlined shape can lead anglers to mistakenly identify it as a shark. Growing to over 50 kg and being common between 10 and 20 kg, cobia is recognised as one of the toughest fighting fish in Australian waters.

Fishing method

Cobia is taken by trolling, jigging or casting lures toward washes and island corners, drifting live baits over offshore reefs or from rocky headlands. Lines should be around 10 to 15, or even up to 24 kg. Traces of 40 to 60-kg nylon will suffice.

Cod, barramundi

Cromileptes altivelis

Also known as humpback cod.

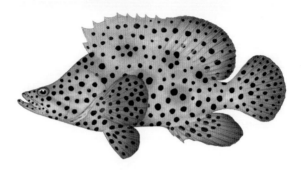

Location/Description

In the head and shoulders, this deep-bodied species closely resembles the barramundi in profile but is a marine fish of the coral reefs. It occurs mainly in caves and crevices to depths of 40 m on the Great Barrier Reef. The barramundi cod grows to 70 cm and 5 kg and is covered in black spots against a cream-grey background. It is sought after by anglers as a fine table fish.

Fishing method

Often caught by anglers fishing for other reef species. Use fresh strip baits and suspend them close to the bottom while drift fishing or at anchor over deep reef. A berley of small cubes will sometimes draw them out. Heavy handlines and hook size from 4/0 to 6/0 are common, and sinker weight is judged on the amount of current running.

Cod, estuary

Epinephelus coioides

Also known as brown-spotted rock cod, greasy cod,
north-west groper.

Location/Description

In Australia the name 'cod' has been
given indiscriminately to a large number
of fish including members of the
Serranidae family. This family has a
number of species, including estuary cod
(*E. coioides*), the most common at around 2 to 4 kg, but
growing in excess of 50 kg. Others include the black
cod (*E. damelli*), the Queensland groper (*E.
lanceolatus*) and the potato cod (*E. tukula*). In New
South Wales, estuary cod, black cod and Queensland
groper are all totally protected.

Fishing method

Cod are common captures in tidal creeks, large inshore bays,
and around some headlands and island groups. A short trace
of heavy nylon or wire is advisable.

Cod, Rankin
Epinephelus multinotatus

Also known as Rankins rock cod.

Location/Description

Rankin cod occur in clear and turbid waters over coral reefs and clear open bottom, from the shore to depths over 90 m. Adults throughout this range use coral and rock outcrops as cover to ambush their prey, a range of bottom fish, crabs and prawns. Juveniles occur mainly on inshore coral reefs. It has been identified as being at risk of over-exploitation from trawling off the Pilbara coast of Western Australia. Rankin cod grow to 1 m and can weigh over 9 kg.

Fishing method

By catch taken by anglers fishing for fish such as red emperor and coral trout. Fresh strip baits fished close to the bottom work well. Most anglers employ heavy handlines and sinkers and use a paternoster style rig with hooks of about 4/0 to 6/0.

Cod, red
Pseudophycis bachus

Also known as bearded rock cod.

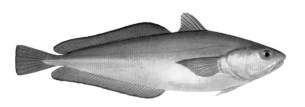

Location/Description

This species is often caught around dusk and at night by anglers fishing at the edges of shallow reefs in sheltered embayments in south-eastern Australia.

Although it may grow to almost 2 kg in weight, most of those caught are less than half that weight. Its nocturnal habits, large mouth, willingness to take a bait and poor fighting qualities often make it a nuisance to anglers fishing for snapper and gummy sharks. Its soft flesh is said to be improved by refrigeration.

Fishing method

Fresh pilchards, fish fillets and squid fished on a running sinker rig with 4/0 hooks is the most common method employed.

Cod, reef

Epinephelus tauvina

Also known as estuarine rock cod, greasy cod, groper.

Location/Description

A non-schooling reef fish, the reef cod occurs in clear coral reef waters. Juveniles prefer shallow tidal pools while solitary adults tend to occur in deeper water down to 300 m. It is one of the most common tropical fish in the group known as rock cod or groper and is often taken by anglers fishing for other species in estuaries and on inshore and offshore reefs. The reef cod grows to over 1 m and can weigh up to 12 kg.

Fishing method

Bottom bouncing with handlines and fresh strip baits accounts for most of the offshore captures. Inshore these fish will take most bait and can be a nuisance for their willingness to attack lures cast at snags for other species.

Dart, swallowtail

Trachinotus coppingeri

Also known as billy lids, dart, surf trevally.

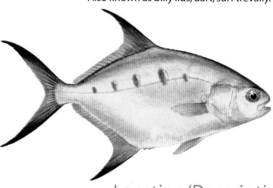

Location/Description

A thin, deep-bodied and agile fish, the swallowtail dart grows to 60 cm in length and is commonly found along surf beaches swimming among the waves with great speed and dexterity. It will snatch at baits, but when hooked, will hang out there with tenacity beyond its size. A relative, the common dart (*T. botla*), is found in Western Australia and a smaller, spotted east coast cousin, the black-spotted dart (*T. bailloni*), has a distribution that overlaps that of the swallowtail.

Fishing method

Dart will take beachworm and pippi baits, or thin strips of fish flesh, and even small lures on occasion. Light beach rods with 3 to 7-kg line are suitable. Cast towards any deep holes adjacent to broken water and move the bait or lure steadily.

Dolphin fish
Coryphaena hippurus

Also known as dollies, dorado, Mahi Mahi.

Location/Description

The dolphin fish, not related to the mammalian dolphin, is one of the most beautiful species of fish; its colours vary from blue to green, and silver to gold. Its dorsal fin stretches from the top of the head to the tail butt, and it has tremendous speed and agility. Preferring warmer waters, it is found northward from Bermagui in the east and from Bunbury in the west. The average size of this species is 2 to 5 kg, but may exceed 25 kg.

Fishing method

Dolphin fish tend to school near reefs or fish aggregating devices such as fish trap buoys, floating objects like rafts, weed, logs or even a length of rope. Troll or cast lures or whole fish baits so they travel past such 'habitats'.

Dory, John

Zeus faber

Also known as St Peter's fish, dories, johnnies.

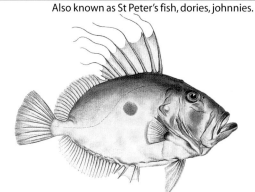

Location/Description

The John dory visits central New South Wales estuaries each winter and becomes an inshore angling target. The related mirror dory (*Zenopsis nebulosus*) and silver dory (*Cyttus australis*) are only obtained by commercial deep trawling. Aside from its habit of taking inshore winter holidays, the John dory can be distinguished from its relatives by a dark 'thumbprint' either side of its body and by the long spines on its dorsal fin. It can grow to about 65 cm in length and weighs about 3 kg – it is one of Australia's best table fish.

Fishing method

Squid strips, fish flesh or live prawns are good, but the best bait is a small live yellowtail suspended under a float on a sharp 3/0 or 4/0 suicide hook. A take is indicated by the float moving out and down steadily.

Drummer, silver

Kyphosus sydneyanus

Also known as buffalo bream.

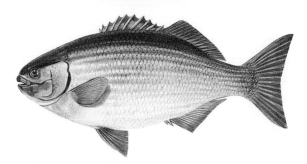

Location/Description

The silver drummer is a streamlined fish with a dull metallic hue. It can grow to about 80 cm and weigh about 12 kg. Often caught from ocean rocks in rough seas, it is quite a brawler when hooked. The popularity of this fish relates to its fighting qualities rather than its table quality. It has relatives such as the western buffalo bream (*K. cornelii*) and the low-finned drummer (*K. vaigiensis*). The silver drummer is very popular in South Australia.

Fishing method

The silver drummer is found around reefs and rocky shores, hence the need to avoid snags and to prevent the fish reaching rocky hideaways when making its run. It is best fished for with a paternoster rig using baits of bread, cunjevoi and abalone gut.

Elephant fish

Callorhinchus milii

Also known as elephant shark.

Location/Description

The elephant fish is actually a shark. The species has recently increased in numbers in inshore coastal waters and embayments in south-eastern Australia. This is most likely to be a side benefit of strengthened controls on the commercial fishery of school and gummy sharks. Growing to about 9 kg, it feeds mainly on shellfish and other soft substrates and has become a popular target species for anglers, particularly in Western Port, Victoria.

Fishing method

Like the gummy shark, elephant fish have no teeth, but the dorsal spine sometimes cuts lines as they roll up in the leader. They are keenly sought by light-tackle anglers. Most are caught on pilchards and fish strips. Use hooks from 2/0 to 3/0 on a running sinker rig.

Emperor, red
Lutjanus sebae

Also known as emperor, government bream, red (juvenile pictured).

Location/Description

Like many prime species of fish, red emperor is vulnerable to fishing pressure and can be quickly fished down to a level where large specimens are difficult to find. It is found often in 30 to 35 m of water on heavy reef structure, where it inhabits the reef edge near the current influence. It is distributed throughout the tropics and is a prized fish of the Great Barrier Reef. It is rarely found in temperate waters. Red emperor is a highly rated table fish commonly caught at sizes of 1 to 6 kg.

Fishing method

Use fresh fillet baits suspended close to the bottom, just off the down-current edge of a fairly vertical shelf of reef. A 10-kg line on a rod is a realistic minimum, with handlines around 40 kg. Sinker weight should suit the current and depth.

Emperor, spangled
Lethrinus nebulosus

Also known as iodine bream, yellow sweetlip, north-west snapper.

Location/Description

A handsome fish with a yellow-golden body with blue spots, the spangled emperor is renowned for its excellent table quality. Average size is from 2 to 3 kg with good specimens reaching 6 kg. Other common emperors are the long-nosed emperor (*L. olivaceous*) and the yellow-tailed emperor (*L. atkinsoni*). The spangled emperor is found in northern waters from northern New South Wales in the east around to southern Western Australia. It prefers a loose rocky bottom of gravel or broken coral and inhabits shallow reefs.

Fishing method

Bottom fishing on anchor with a paternoster rig and cut baits is best. The fish will occasionally strike at jigs worked near the bottom. Best baits include fish, crabs, prawns and squid.

Flathead, dusky

Platycephalus fuscus

Also known as black flathead, flatty, lizard.

Location/Description

Of the fourteen common species of flathead in Australian waters, the largest by far is the dusky flathead. This elongated fish takes its name from the colour of its head. It is common in estuaries along the east coast from around the Whitsundays in Queensland to as far south as Victoria. Growing to 15 kg, it is more commonly encountered from 1 to 3 kg. The dusky flathead is a bottom dweller, usually found in shallow water (1 to 6 m) in estuaries, bays and surf beaches.

Fishing method

From a boat with drift baits of fish strip or whole prawns, rigged to bounce along the bottom behind a sinker heavy enough to stir up sediment. From shore, flick out into deep channels and allow the tide to sweep the bait around. It responds well to lures or saltwater flies.

Flathead, sand (northern)

Platycephalus arenarius

Also known as flagtail flathead.

Location/Description

While it is a mainly tropical species, the northern sand flathead has a lot in common with its southern counterpart in terms of its significance to anglers. For example, it grows to about 46 cm and 5 kg, is commonly taken by anglers in inshore waters, bays and estuaries, and is an excellent eating fish. Young sand flathead tend to school, often resting and leaving their imprints on shallow sand banks. The distinctive horizontal black and white bands on the tail give this species its alternative name – flagtail flathead.

Fishing method

A common capture, northern sand flathead will take most baits including fish strips, prawns and live bait. Fish with a running sinker and 2/0 to 4/0 hooks, and allow the bait to move across the seabed. This fish is a common capture on small-style lures and saltwater flies.

Flathead, sand (southern)

Platycephalus bassensis

Also known as bay flathead, sandy, channel rat.

Location/Description

This is the main 'bread-and-butter' species of anglers fishing over sand and mud bottoms in bays and coastal waters of Victoria and Tasmania. Although it grows to 50 cm in length and approaches 2 kg in weight, most of those taken measure 25–35 cm. Having a wide mouth, the flathead will attempt to swallow large baits intended for snapper and other fish. Anglers frequently say they are trying to catch more challenging species, but most agree there's nothing they'd rather eat than 'flatties'.

Fishing method

Southern sand flathead is probably the most commonly caught saltwater fish in south-east Australia. Bottom fishing with a paternoster-style rig and allowing the boat to drift while raising and lowering the bait is an effective method. Will take most bait including pilchards, fish strips and squid.

Flathead, southern blue-spot
Platycephalus speculator

Also known as yank flathead, long nose,
sandies, shovel nose.

Location/Description

This fish inhabits the Victorian coast-
line from New South Wales to South
Australia, and also the waters of northern
Tasmania and southern Western Australia. The southern blue-spot species
resembles the dusky in appearance and occupies a
similar range of habitats. It is commonly caught by
drift fishing over sand and it is distinguished by the
dark bars across its back. In Port Phillip Bay, Victoria,
it is the predominant 'larger' specimen caught. It is an
excellent table fish.

Fishing method

Strip baits of fish, prawns, whole small fish, etc. are best, but
lures will also work. Mostly caught by boat anglers, but land-
based anglers can cast baits into bankside channels and
across weed beds in southern estuaries.

Flathead, toothy
Neoplatycephalus aurimaculatus

Also known as yellowfinned flathead.

Location/Description

The toothy flathead occurs in open coastal and offshore waters throughout Bass Strait, around Tasmania and off South Australia where it is very popular among anglers. They commonly fish for it at depths of 40–50 m. It is often confused with tiger or trawl flathead (*N. richardsoni*) which has an overlapping distribution from eastern Tasmania to Sydney. Both species have large canine teeth, occur to depths of 160 m, and grow to lengths of 60 cm and 3 kg in weight.

Fishing method

This species is most commonly caught over offshore sand flats. Drift fishing using a paternoster rig, 2/0 to 4/0 long-shank hooks and strip baits is a successful method. Due to their teeth, leaders of about 15 kg breaking strain are recommended.

Flounder, small-toothed

Pseudorhombus jenysii

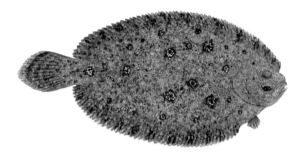

Location/Description

The flounder begins life with an eye on each side of its head, but metamorphoses into adulthood with both eyes on the same side. The small-toothed flounder is found in both eastern and Western Australia, is dark coloured and carries five to six eye-like blotches spread around the body. Other species include the large-toothed, elongated, long-snouted and green-back flounders. They are common in southern esturaries and are considered to be fine table fish.

Fishing method

Flounder may be speared in some States, but are usually caught with lines from 2 to 4 kg, small long-shank hooks and small pieces of bait, fished on the bottom from a drifting boat. Popular baits include fish strips, peeled prawn, marine worms or whitebait.

Garfish, eastern sea

Hyporhamphus australis

Also known as garie, beakie, red beak.

Location/Description

The slender, bony sea garfish is a common species on the east coast, targeted both for bait and food. The flesh, despite its small size and large number of bones, is keenly sought for its outstanding flavour. A southern form, *H. melanochir*, is similar in all respects to *H. australis* but grows larger, to the delight of South Australian and Victorian anglers. The garfish is found around jetties and other estuary and bay structures, and is most active in the summer and autumn months.

Fishing method

Sea garfish can be readily line-caught, and are also netted professionally. To catch garfish, berley with bran or bread, and use small baits of fish or prawn flesh (or dough) on No. 6 to 8 long-shank hooks on a float rig.

Groper, baldchin

Choerodon rubescens

Also called Venus tuskfish, blue parrot.

Location/Description

The baldchin groper is found on coral reefs and rock and weed areas on the central coast of Western Australia. Like many other species of territorial reef fish that are targeted by anglers for their excellent eating qualities, it is considered vulnerable to localised depletion and overfishing. Most of those caught by anglers are taken during summer and autumn at sizes from 40 cm to over 60 cm, although it grows to 90 cm and over 6 kg.

Fishing method

Baldchin gropers are caught mainly on baits such as squid and fish strips fished on the bottom over inshore reefs. Use a paternoster rig and hooks from about 2/0 to 4/0. Smaller fish move inshore over tidal flats and can be sight-fished with lures and flies.

Groper, blue
Achoerodus viridis

Also known as bluey.

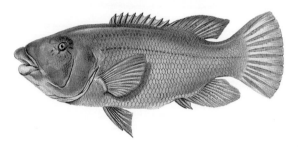

Location/Description

The eastern blue groper inhabits the waters of mid-Queensland and New South Wales and commonly grows to around 15 kg. A western species, *A. gouldii*, also exists, distributed from South Australia around into Western Australia, and can grow in excess of 30 kg. The western female is greenish, the eastern is reddish brown (called red groper), and the juveniles of both are a grey-brown in colour.

Fishing method

To withstand the tug of war involved in landing a groper, use heavy line, extra strong hooks from 1/0 to 6/0, large flavoured baits of cunjevoi, red crab or abalone gut, and a powerful rod. The fish is usually caught by land-based fishing from rocks.

Gurnard, red
Chelidonichthys kumu

Also known as flying gurnard.

Location/Description

This is one of several Australian gurnards featuring fan-like pectoral fins marked with iridescent blue markings. It reaches lengths of 50 cm, has firm tasty flesh and is often caught with flathead in depths over 10 m. Also commonly called 'gurnards' are the gurnard perches, several of which are caught in coastal waters around southern Australia. While most are good eating, they are notorious for their strong venomous spines and most anglers prefer to cut them free rather than risk bringing them into the boat.

Fishing method

Red gurnard are mainly caught as a by-catch by anglers fishing for other bottom species including snapper and flathead. Gurnard will take most strip baits including pilchard, squid and fish fillets. Use a paternoster rig, 4/0 hooks, and drift-fish over rubble ground.

Hairtail
Trichiurus lepturus

Also known as Australian hairtail, Cox's hairtail, largerhead hairtail.

Location/Description

The hairtail is a long fish with a fearsomely toothed head, a scaleless body and a tail tapering to a thin, thread-like end. The body colour is a brilliant silver, like polished chrome. This fish is found in coastal bays and estuaries of Australia's east and west coasts. Growing in excess of 2 m and weighing over 4 kg as an adult, the hairtail is most active at night. Usually found in deep holes in estuaries, but unpredictable as to when it will bite, it provides exciting sport for anglers.

Fishing method

Most regular hairtail anglers use from 4 to 10-kg line, a 1/0 to 4/0 hook, and always with a short (15-cm) wire trace as insurance against those teeth. Favoured baits include fillet of yellowtail or slimy mackerel and whole or half pilchards.

Hapuku

Polyprion oxygeneios

Also known as New Zealand groper, hapuka

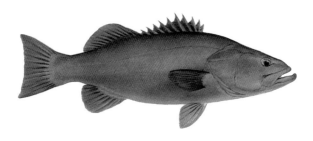

Location/Description

The extension of recreational line fishing onto the continental shelf has given anglers access to species that combine large size with excellent eating qualities. The hapuku and the less common bass groper (*P. americanus*) are two such species. Growing to 1.8 m and around 80 kg, they are taken on pinnacles and drop-offs at depths of 100–400 m. Anglers are increasingly fishing for these species off southern NSW, Tasmania's east coast and south-eastern South Australia where the continental shelf is close to land.

Fishing method

Anglers fishing the deep drop-offs along the continental shelf are most likely to encounter this species. To land them you will need a gunnel-mounted winch and 2 kg of lead weight to get your bait down through currents to the depths. Hapuku will take most fresh fish strips and squid. Hooks size from 6/0 to 8/0 is the norm.

Herring, oxeye
Megalops cyprinoides

Also known as tarpon.

Location/Description

Found in tropical water, from far northern New South Wales, throughout Queensland and across the Gulf of Carpentaria to the Northern Territory, this species is an active, shiny, large-scaled fish, mostly silver in colour, and a great lure and fly taker. It provides a light-tackle diversion for anglers taking a break from barramundi and saratoga. Oxeye are commonly fished for sport as they are very fast and resist until exhausted. It is not highly regarded for its table quality and is usually released unharmed.

Fishing method

Best caught using casting lures, especially small lead-headed jigs with either feather, fibre or soft plastic tails. Larger specimens will take small swimming plugs and small surface poppers are also particularly useful, whether cast with fly tackle or spinning gear.

Hussar
Lutjanus adetii

Location/Description

A common species of rocky and coral reefs and broken bottom on the southern Queensland coast, the hussar often occurs in large schools during the day, dispersing at night to feed, usually on the bottom. Bright pink in colour, it has a yellow stripe running from head to tail. While it grows to 50 cm, most of those caught are around 30 cm. It is a good table fish but is often considered a nuisance as it interferes with fishing targeted at other species of reef fish.

Fishing method

Bottom bouncing over reefs with strip baits using a paternoster rig is the most common method. Use a handline, and plan to catch bigger fish. Hussars are a willing fish, attacking lures as readily as they do fresh fish strips in some areas.

Jack, mangrove
Lutjanus argentimaculatus

Also known as creek red bream, dog bream, red bream, jack, mangrove snapper, rock barramundi.

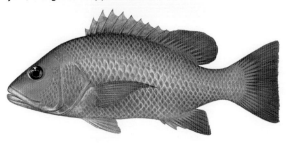

Location/Description

Mangrove jack is common throughout the tropical north, as far south as Coffs Harbour in the east and Exmouth in the west. A dark red, powerfully built fish, mangrove jack up to 3 kg are prevalent in tidal creeks and estuaries. Larger fish tend to move out into bays and on to onshore reefs. Some monster specimens of 11 kg or more have been taken from offshore reefs in New South Wales. A good table fish, it should not be confused with red bass, which has a distinctive 'pit' in front of each eye and is often toxic.

Fishing method

Mangrove jack has canine teeth, sharp spines and gill blades. It lives around oyster-encrusted rocks, mangrove roots and various other line-cutting structures. Line classes upwards of 6 kg are adequate. The fish will hit lures, baits or flies, then dash for cover.

Javelin fish

Pomadasys kaakan

Also known as barred grunter, trumpeter, spotted grunter,
spotted javelin fish.

Location/Description

This fish's other common name,
grunter, evolved because of its habit of
emitting loud grunting sounds on
capture. The name 'javelin fish' comes
from the heavy spear-like anal fin that is
capable of inflicting severe wounds on anglers who
handle this fish carelessly. Commonly found in
estuarine rivers, especially close to the sea, javelin fish
live in far northern New South Wales, Queensland,
the Northern Territory and parts of Western Australia.
This fish is great table fare and good sport on
reasonable tackle.

Fishing method

Fish strips or prawn baits are best. Most anglers fish with 6 to
10-kg tackle and just enough sinker weight to get the bait down
in a tidal run. Because the javelin often lives near line-cutting
structures, a heavier trace of about 25 kg is sometimes used.

Jewfish, black
Protonibea diacanthus

Also known as spotted croaker, spotted jewfish, croaker.

Location/Description

A fish of northern waters, especially within the Northern Territory, the black jewfish is a darker coloured member of the same family as the southern mulloway. It also carries scattered dark blotches over much of its body. It has a predilection for reef areas, sunken wrecks and deepwater wharves in northern harbours. This fish grows to about 1.5 m and can weigh about 16 kg. A predator of the first order, this fish loves nothing more than a large live bait (half a kilo is not too big). It is caught by dropping baits down and hanging on.

Fishing method

Use heavy handlines on normal gear, as the runs, when they come, are short and sizzling, and you either stop your fish or lose it. Rod and reel fishing is possible, but usually only when the fish have congregated over a relatively clear space of bottom.

Jewfish, little

Johnius vogleri

Also known as silver jewfish.

Location/Description

The little jewfish, reaching just 30 cm in length, is smaller than its two heavyweight relatives, the mulloway and the black jewfish. It is often mistaken for a juvenile mulloway but there are distinguishing features, notably that the little jewfish is always fatter for a given length than the southern mulloway. The little jewfish is significantly lighter in colour and lacks the dark blotches of the black jewfish as well. *J. vogleri* is found in deep holes or near vertical structures such as wharves or bridges, in northern latitudes only.

Fishing method

Use live baits of mullet, herring or prawns in tropical rivers and creeks. A running sinker rig with a large slab bait can be almost as effective, particularly if taken from a freshly caught mullet or pike.

Jewfish, Westralian
Glaucosoma hebraicum

Also known as dhufish, jewie, West Australian jewfish.

Location/Description

Related to the pearl perch of eastern Australia, this magnificent table fish is much larger, lives in generally deeper water and is the sole province of lucky Western Australian anglers – hence its common name. It is generally confined to coastal waters between Shark Bay and the beginnings of the Great Australian Bight, and so is unfamiliar to most eastern anglers. Anglers fishing the east coast would think they had died and gone to heaven if they hauled in one of these, which can grow to 26 kg.

Fishing method

Stout handlines with a lot of sinker weight in the rig, and preferably lines with minimal stretch, are best. Use fish strip baits, skinned octopus or squid, if absolutely fresh. Change baits every so often if there are no bites – freshness is that important!

Job-fish, rosy
Pristipomoides filamentosus

Also known as king snapper, rosy snapper.

Location/Description

Plentiful within the warmer waters of Queensland and far northern New South Wales, the rosy Job-fish is also caught around Lord Howe Island and off Australia's north-western continental shelf. Growing in excess of 7 kg, it is a handsome, top-grade table species, with the same colouration as adult snapper, but much more streamlined. Related to the small-toothed Job-fish (*Aphareus furca*) and green Job-fish (*Aprion viriscens*), it is known for its sad look and hence the biblical reference in its common name.

Fishing method

Fished for over reefs in 50 m depth or more, the rosy Job-fish bites best on cut fish baits at night and is an excellent table fish, as are all Job-fish. Solid tackle with 10-kg line or heavier is useful due to the depth of water it inhabits.

Kingfish, yellowtail

Seriola lalandi

Also known as bandit, hoodlum, king.

Location/Description

A fish of exciting power and glamorous appearance, it has the nasty habit of taking lures and bait rigs and refusing to give them back. This very popular sport fish can be caught off the rocks or from a boat. It is usually associated with reef areas and often schools. It is found in waters from southern Queensland to New South Wales, Victoria, South Australia and as far west as Shark Bay in Western Australia. Growing to 50 kg or better, this species averages from 4 to 10 kg.

Fishing method

Use lures, strip baits, cube baits or live baits, fished over reef, around deepwater wharf pylons and channel markers, from boats or the ocean rocks. Berley works well. The selection of a breaking strain in line should reflect the size and strength of the fish.

Leatherjacket, six-spine
Meuschenia freycineti

Location/Description

This leatherjacket is inclined to suck on bait and bite off hooks. It is popular among anglers and spear fishers for its size, attractive blue and yellow markings, and good eating qualities. While colouration and markings vary with size, sex, and location around the coast, the main distinguishing feature is the group of five to eight large spines near the base of the tail. As with all leatherjackets, this species also has a prominent dorsal spine above the eyes. It inhabits shallow rocky reefs and grows to around 50 cm and 3 kg.

Fishing method

Often caught by whiting anglers, the six-spine leatherjacket will take baits such as sandworms, mussels and pippis. It is usually fished just off the bottom or in midwater. Long-shank hooks in size 6 to 4 should be employed. The six-spine leatherjacket is common around wharves and channel marker beacons that have become overgrown with weed and shellfish.

Leatherjacket, toothbrush
Acanthaluteres vittiger

Also known as jackets, pale brown leatherjacket.

Location/Description

The prominent dorsal spine above the eyes of this species folds completely into a groove when not in use. Its other distinguishing feature is the leathery skin rather than scales. It is a peaceful breed of fish that mooches around reef and weed beds grazing daintily with its small but chisel-toothed mouth. The toothbrush leatherjacket, which grows to about 32 cm, is commonly found around southern Australia, from Coffs Harbour, New South Wales, to Western Australia's Jurien Bay.

Fishing method

The shearing teeth make long-shank hooks necessary. Baits should be small and soft, such as peeled prawn, fish flesh, skinned octopus or squid meat. An unweighted or lightly weighted bait allowed to sink slowly is the best method.

Ling, rock
Genypterus tigerinus

Also known as ling.

Location/Description

An excellent eating fish, the rock ling can attain 9 kg in weight, but has been depleted in numbers over much of its range by a combination of line fishing, spear fishing, gill-netting and trawling.

It occurs on reefs where it usually spends the day in holes or caves, leaving to feed over reefs and nearby weed or seagrass beds and broken bottom at night. Because of its shape, size, colour, and reef-dwelling habits, the ling is often confused with the conger eel. When hooked it shares the eel's habit of knotting and contorting itself trying to escape.

Fishing method

A by-catch of southern-bay snapper by anglers fishing at night, the ling is a bottom feeder and shows a distinct preference for fresh bait including fish strips, pilchards and squid. Use a running sinker rig and 4/0 hooks.

Long tom, slender
Strongylura leiura

Also known as hornpike long tom, needlefish.

Location/Description

The long tom has jaws of equal length, studded with rows of tiny, needle-sharp teeth. The slender long tom grows to 1.2 m and is distinguished by the black bar on the side of the head. It is found in Australia's northern and temperate waters, and is related to the barred long tom (*Ablennes hians*), which is purely tropical, the stout long tom (*Tylosurus gavialoides*) and the crocodilian long tom (*Tylosurus crocodilus*), the last two being much larger fish and found in the same waters.

Fishing method

Long tom are surface cruisers, preying on small fish which they herd and slash at in spectacular fashion. They are easy to draw strikes from with small lures but not so simple to hook, there being little soft tissue among all those teeth.

Luderick

Girella tricuspidata

Also known as blackfish, darkie, nigger.

Location/Description

A fish of the estuaries and inshore rocks mainly along the eastern seaboard, luderick is most commonly found in New South Wales. This chunky little fish is usually encountered around a half to 1.5 kg. Essentially vegetarian, the luderick will take baits of marine worms, prawns and nippers on occasion. A good table fish if prepared correctly, it is often kept alive in net bags, then bled, cleaned and skinned immediately before the angler leaves for home.

Fishing method

Float fishing is best with green weed or sea lettuce baits from the ocean rocks, river breakwalls or within estuaries from bank or boat. The float is weighted with either running barrels, beans or crimped split shot, and hooks should be small.

Mackerel, grey
Scomberomorus semifasciatus

Also known as broad-barred Spanish mackerel, greys, broad-bars.

Location/Description

The grey mackerel occurs around coastal headlands and on rocky reefs to depths of 100 m off northern Australia. It has a deeper body than other mackerels, with a characteristic dark green back and vertical markings, and grows to 120 cm and 8 kg. Its colours fade to grey after capture, hence its name. It feeds on small pelagic fish and is generally taken by anglers as a light game-fish species targeted in murky inshore waters. It is not noted for its fighting qualities.

Fishing method

Most are caught trolling lures and baits, and on floating baits allowed to drift down around rocky outcrops. Wire leader should be employed and hook size should suit bait, but about 4/0 to 6/0 will cover most situations. Occasionally anglers have the opportunity to cast high speed lures at schooling fish breaking the surface.

Mackerel, school

Scomberomorus queenslandicus

Also known as doggies.

Location/Description

A common species of Queensland and Northern Territory waters, the school mackerel is one of the smaller mackerel species and often mixes with other mackerels in surface schools. During winter and spring schools move into inshore waters, bays and estuaries where the fish is highly regarded as a light game species because of its fighting qualities. It is also highly rated as a table fish. Growing to over 8 kg, most are taken at 2–4 kg.

Fishing method

The school mackerel is a light tackle sport fish, rated a nuisance at times. Most are caught trolling small lures and fly casting. Will readily attack fish strips and can be berleyed and held near the boat for some fast, light tackle action. Use wire leader and hooks of about 4/0.

Mackerel, shark
Grammatorcynus bicarinatus

Also known as large-scaled tuna, scaly mackerel, sharkie.

Location/Description

The southern limits to the distribution of this tropical species are around Fraser Island in the east and Geographe Bay, near Busselton, in the west. Shark mackerel comprises much of the Western Australian rock angler's catch on lures north of Shark Bay. Usual shark mackerel sizes are from 2 to 6 kg, but can double that. Whole (up to 12 kg in size), it is a prized trolling bait for giant marlin off Cairns. A distinguishing feature of the shark mackerel is its double lateral line. It takes its name from the shark-like smell when gutted.

Fishing method

Lure casting from ocean rocks is best in Western Australia. Trolling around inner reef edges is best from about Gladstone north. They respond to either lures or baits of garfish, mullet and pike. Suitable line classes are from 4 to 8 kg; wire trace is essential.

Mackerel, slimy

Scomber australasicus

Also known as blue mackerel, common mackerel, slimies.

Location/Description

This speedy little baitfish is excellent live or cut bait for larger quarry such as snapper, mulloway, yellowtail kingfish and tuna. Usually caught from 15 to 25 cm in length, this species prefers cooler areas and often forms extensive surface shoals. It is most common inshore in the southern half of Australia, where it schools over reefs, around islands and headlands, and occasionally enters bays. Its skin is soft and slippery to touch – hence its common name.

Fishing method

Light handlines or flick rods are used to cast tiny metal lures or flies, small pieces of cut bait or multi-hook live-bait jigs. These fish respond to berley and can be kept alive in a large container of sea water, provided the water is constantly exchanged.

Mackerel, Spanish

Scomberomorus commerson

Also known as narrow-barred mackerel, narrow-barred
Spanish mackerel, Spaniards, Spanish.

Location/Description

The largest member of the mackerel
family and a fast swimming oceanic
species, the Spanish mackerel can grow
to 30 kg or more but is commonly
encountered around 5 to 10 kg. It ranges
throughout the tropics and as far south as Montague
Island on the east coast and Rottnest Island in the west.
A streamlined fish, it is all about speed and slicing
power. Its serrated rows of dagger-like teeth interlock
like shears. It is an extremely popular game fish and
fair table food.

Fishing method

Mackerel teeth mean wire traces are a must, or at least ganged
hooks. Mackerel can be trolled, or spun to with lures, especially
surface poppers. They love live baits as well, and dead baits are
useful. Mackerel usually hit first to maim the bait then come
back to inhale it.

Mackerel, spotted

Scomberomorus munroi

Also known as Japanese mackerel, snook, spottie,
Australian spotted mackerel.

Location/Description

As its common name indicates, numerous small spots on its body distinguish this species. The spotted mackerel frequents a similar area to Spanish mackerel although it rarely moves further south than Forster, on the New South Wales coast. Slightly smaller than the Spaniard, it averages around 3 to 5 kg, with a really big fish being around 8 or 9 kg and probably coming from a north Queensland offshore reef. Found offshore in schools, its presence is usually signalled by wheeling and diving birds.

Fishing method

Trolling lures or live baits, or drifting with live or cut baits over inshore plateaus of reefs is best. Mackerel teeth mean wire trace is essential or at least ganged hooks. This fish will often move up a berley trail behind an anchored boat.

Marlin, black
Makaira indica

Also known as black, silver marlin, silver.

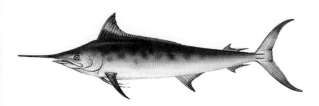

Location/Description

Black marlin is a fast swimming, highly prized game fish that grows to more than 4.5 m and can weigh about 700 kg. Found offshore right down the east and west coasts, black marlin becomes less common the further south you go. In Queensland and much of New South Wales, marlin of various sizes are regular summer visitors to waters as shallow as 40 m or less. Many game fishers suspect big fish inhabit deeper offshore trenches year round. The largest known aggregation of giant black marlin is around the Great Barrier Reef north of Cairns.

Fishing method

Giant black marlin of 500 kg are taken trolling large baits well offshore. Smaller blacks, around 100 kg, are regularly taken closer inshore. Boat anglers troll large skirted lures, bibless minnows or whole fish baits – either dead or alive.

Marlin, blue
Makaira nigricans

Also known as blues, Indo-Pacific blue marlin.

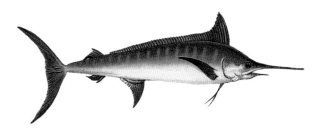

Location/Description

The blue marlin inhabits much the same waters as the black marlin but is less common and appears to prefer the deep, oceanic currents and to be more tolerant of cooler temperatures. Blue marlin can grow to more than 900 kg and have been caught as far south as Storm Bay in Tasmania. It is a prized game fish, and some anglers consider it a tougher opponent than equivalent sized black marlin. Large blue marlin have been captured offshore of Bermagui, south of Sydney. Once hooked, a marlin of any size will put up a tremendous fight.

Fishing method

Lure fishing works best, especially over deep offshore canyons where the bigger fish prowl. Lures need to be large, as do the rods, reels and line classes, because when hooked, big blue marlin are capable of stripping over 1000 m of line from a reel.

Marlin, striped
Tetrapturus audax

Also known as stripey.

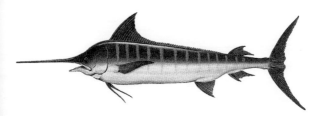

Location/Description

Far more prevalent along the eastern seaboard than in the west, the striped marlin is generally a lighter built fish than either the black or blue of the same length and weighs up to 200 kg. It makes up for this lack of bulk by being the most spectacular of all the billfish when hooked, often racing across the sea making immense leaps. It is not unknown for an adult striped marlin to jump more than thirty times during a fight, and twenty consecutive jumps are common. It takes its name from the bluish stripes that extend across its body.

Fishing method

Small trolled live baits, such as slimy mackerel and yellowtail, are favoured. Trolling an array of skirted lures intended for blue marlin will often land this fish. It will respond to live baits cast across its path when cruising the surface.

Milkfish
Chanos chanos

Also known as giant herring, Moreton Bay salmon.

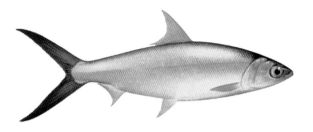

Location/Description

The milkfish is a tropical species found swimming in schools in coastal waters near reefs and in the open waters of estuaries and mangrove shores. It is bright silver with a large, distinctively forked tail and a single short dorsal fin. A powerful swimmer that grows to 1.2 m and over 10 kg, it is considered an outstanding sport fish. Unfortunately, its fighting qualities are not matched by its eating qualities which are rated as very poor.

Fishing method

An occasional by-catch of fly fishers working tropical sand flats; most milkfish are caught on small baits of fish pieces and lures. Use small hooks and hide them in the bait with just the point exposed. When there are reasonable numbers about they can be attracted by the scent of berley.

Moonfish
Zabidius novemaculeatus

Also known as moony, short-finned batfish.

Location/Description

This exceptionally deep and round-bodied fish occurs in schools in coastal waters to depths of 40 m. It is especially abundant around coral reefs, wharves and other structures, and in estuaries. The moonfish has a very small mouth and is silver, with two dark vertical bars running through the eye and operculum. Growing to 45 cm and around 2 kg, it provides good sport when taken on light gear and is a good table fish.

Fishing method

Moonfish are caught on bait fished on the bottom. Productive baits include small fish pieces, prawns and squid. Use a paternoster rig, small hooks about size 4, and light tackle to get the most sport out of this increasingly rare species.

Saltwater

Morwong, blue
Nemadactylus douglasii

Also known as grey morwong, mowie.

Location/Description

Commonly found throughout the inshore coastal reef waters of southern Queensland, all of New South Wales and the eastern part of Victoria, the blue morwong is also an occasional catch in Tasmania's warmer northern waters. A fish that can grow to 90 cm and weigh 11 kg, the blue morwong favours moderately deep reef areas and rubble bottom, and is a popular charter-boat fish for handline anglers bouncing baits off the bottom. While not highly rated as a sporting fish, despite its size and fight, it is a fair table fish.

Fishing method

It is best caught with baits of fish strip and peeled prawn, fished as close to the vertical edges of reefs as is practicable. As charter boats drift-fish, such precision is not always achieved, but anglers in charge of their own craft should do a better job.

Morwong, jackass
Nemadactylus macropterus

Also known as perch, jackass fish, terakihi.

Location/Description

While larger fish occur mainly on smooth bottom on the continental shelf and upper slope, where they are trawled, smaller fish of up to 500 g are often hooked over inshore reefs and around piers and breakwaters in bays in south-eastern Australia. A schooling fish, the jackass morwong has firm white flesh with a mild pleasant flavour and grows to 70 cm and 4.5 kg. It is particularly valued by Tasmanian anglers as an alternative to sand flathead and red cod.

Fishing method

Fish with bait such as craytail, pilchards, fish strips or squid. Use a paternoster rig and keep bait on or near the bottom. Hook size should be from No. 2 to 4/0. Most are caught drifting over reefs, with many anglers preferring to fish for them with handlines.

Morwong, red
Cheilodactylus fuscus

Also known as sea carp.

Location/Description

Like other morwong species, the red morwong is an attractive fish of good eating qualities taken by anglers (and spear fishers) fishing over coastal reefs. It is often found in large schools and occurs at depths down to 30 m. It grows to 65 cm and 4 kg and can be distinguished readily from the similar banded morwong (C. *spectabilis*) by the presence of two small 'horns' in front of its eyes and its more uniform red-brown upper body colouration.

Fishing method

As with jackass morwong, red morwong is a reef species. Fish on the bottom with a paternoster rig and use bait such as craytail, pilchards, fish strips or squid. Hook size should be from No. 2 to 4/0. Most are caught drifting over reefs, with many anglers preferring to fish for them with handlines.

Mullet, red
Upeneichthys vlamingii

Also known as goatfish.

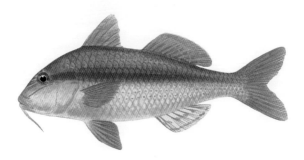

Location/Description

The red mullet readily sheds its large scales when handled. It is often caught on light reef or among seagrass or weed beds. Most red mullet taken by anglers are released because of their small size (20–30 cm) and soft flesh. However, this is one of a family of very similar species known around the world and highly valued, particularly around the Mediterranean Sea. Consequently, Australians from southern European countries prize them. Several other red mullet species occur around Australia.

Fishing method

An unusually colourful species, and quite common, red mullet are generally caught by anglers fishing sand patches between seagrasses for whiting. Use a light outfit, running sinker rig, No. 6 long-shank hooks, and baits including sandworms, pippis and mussel.

Mullet, sand
Myxus elongatus

Also known as lano, sandie, tallegalane.

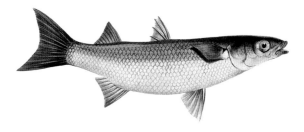

Location/Description

The sand mullet is widespread through-out New South Wales and South Australia, and occasionally in southern Western Australia. Growing to 38 cm in length and weighing about 900 g, it is a solid-bodied streamlined fish with a straight back, large eye and small, pointed snout. It also has a large black spot at the base of the pectoral fin and rows of well-developed teeth uncharacteristic of the mullet family. Caught mostly from sand flat areas in estuaries or from beaches, sand mullet is excellent bait for larger fish, but also a good table fish.

Fishing method

Small baits of fish flesh, peeled prawn, marine worms or dough are best. These can be fished on the bottom or unweighted, but more success will be enjoyed if you berley heavily with bread and fish these baits under a slim quill-float. Hooks should be small.

Mullet, sea
Mugil cephalus

Also known as bully mullet, hardgut mullet, poddy mullet, grey mullet.

Location/Description

The sea mullet is a much larger mullet than most, growing to an astonishing 8 kg or more, but is rarely seen above 2 kg. It is a temperate species of fish that spends part of its life in freshwater reaches of coastal rivers and lakes. It travels to sea as an adult and runs up the east coast in huge schools for annual spawning. The eggs are carried southwards until the young have developed enough to enter bays and harbours. These mullet are a common catch in coastal rivers of New South Wales.

Fishing method

Float fishing in estuaries is best, or fishing baits on the bottom in either estuaries or surf. It forages in freshwater reaches of rivers over weed beds, but can be caught on small trout flies. It is not easy to tempt and is rarely taken by line in Western Australia.

Mullet, yelloweye
Aldrichetta forsteri

Also known as pilch.

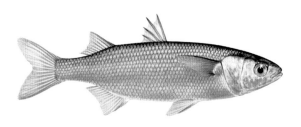

Location/Description

A similar fish to sand mullet, but growing to 40 cm in length and weighing about 950 g, this species is distinguished by a rounder back, absence of the black spot near the pectoral fins, and having large, prominent yellow eyes. It shares similar distribution to the sand mullet, but is found much further west. In Western Australia it is known as 'pilch', and is taken from both estuary and surf. The yelloweye mullet is predominant in Victoria where it is a major part of the surf angling catch. It is a good table fish, with firm white fillets ideal for cooking.

Fishing method

In the surf the paternoster rig is best using small pieces of fresh tuna, or better still, pippis, mussel or other shell baits. The yelloweye mullet responds well to berley and is found in gutters close to shore and in estuaries.

Mulloway

Argyrosomus hololepidotus

Also known as butterfish, jew, jewie, jewfish,
river kingfish, soapie (juvenile).

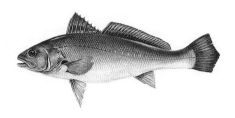

Location/Description

Known by a host of confusing names,
this large species is a predator of major
southern estuarine river and lake
systems, surf beaches and offshore reefs.
Growing in excess of 50 kg, most adult
mulloway are caught between 10 and 15 kg. The
smaller juveniles, up to 4 kg, are known as 'soapies'
because of their soft flesh. They will often follow
squid and sometimes develop a fixation for them. The
mulloway is considered an important sport fish and
respected for its table quality, particularly in South
Australia.

Fishing method

Use strip baits in the surf and live baits of pike, yellowtail scad,
slimy mackerel or mullet in estuaries or over reefs. Hooks
should be 5/0 to 8/0, lines from 6 to 10 kg, but over reefs or
from the rocks, 15 to 20-kg line may be more sensible.
Mulloway will also take lures.

Nannygai

Centroberyx affinis

Also known as 'gai, goat (nanny-goat), nanny, redfish.

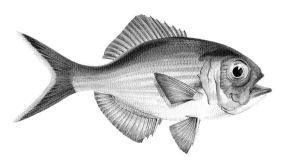

Location/Description

A deepwater species found in New South Wales, Victoria and Tasmania, the nannygai is a prime commercial fish occasionally caught by anglers fishing deep reefs for snapper or morwong. The nannygai is conspicuous by its colouring, which is deep pink to red with metallic-silvery tints. An acceptable to good table fish, growing over 2 kg but being common at about half that size, nannygai is also a prized live bait for yellowfin tuna. A similar species, the red snapper (*C. gerrardi*), is found in southern waters.

Fishing method

Strip baits of fish flesh mounted on hooks from 1/0 to 4/0 are best, as this small fish has a large mouth. Rigs are commonly of the paternoster type, with a large sinker hung below several short dropper lines, each carrying its own hook and bait.

Perch, estuary

Macquaria colonorum

Also known as Australian perch, freshwater perch, perch.

Location/Description

Estuary perch is found in the brackish reaches of coastal fresh water from around Lismore in New South Wales, down the southern New South Wales and Victorian coast and around to the Murray mouth in South Australia. Some isolated populations also exist in northern Tasmania. Similar to bass (*M. novemaculata*) in appearance and habit, this fish will be found near snags, creek mouths, reefs and rock-wall structures in mid to upper estuarine sections of coastal rivers. Estuary perch can grow to about 60 cm and weigh about 10 kg.

Fishing method

The perch loves baits of live prawns, crickets, worms, tiny mullet and crabs, but will occasionally take trolled or cast lures and flies. Its activity is quite tide-related, and tide changes at either dawn or dusk are prime fishing times.

Perch, Moses

Lutjanus russelli

Also known as Moses sea perch, Moses snapper, black-spot sea perch.

Location/Description

The Moses perch is a similar fish to fingermark and is often confused with it. Found around inshore reefs and mangroves in tropical estuaries, it is more prevalent across the top of Australia. It is usually found in pairs or small groups, sometimes hiding under ledges or gutters. The Moses perch is reasonably small, averaging between 400 g and 1.5 kg, and is frequently considered a nuisance fish by amateur anglers hoping to catch larger fish.

Fishing method

Moses perch can be caught on lures and with both dead and live bait. Lures cast close to mangroves and meant for barramundi or mangrove jack can induce strikes from Moses perch.

Perch, pearl
Glaucosoma scapulare

Also known as eastern pearl perch, pearlie, nannygai.

Location/Description

This species frequents offshore deep water over rubble beds and low reef areas. It is found from central Queensland through northern New South Wales, to as far south as Newcastle. Those caught usually average around 1 to 2 kg. It has a deep, laterally compressed body, large eye and a black-skinned bony extension to the top of the gill cover. Beneath the thin black membrane the bony plate is pearly – hence its common name. It is widely regarded as one of Australia's best table fish.

Fishing method

Only fresh fish-strip baits are likely to be taken, or small squid. Hooks of 3/0 to 6/0 are suitable, with lines usually being 4 to 8 kg on rods and 15 to 20 kg for handlines.

Perch, stripey sea

Lutjanus carponotatus

Also known as stripey snapper, stripey.

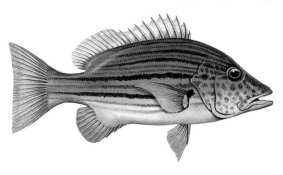

Location/Description

Also known as stripey, this species has brown and yellow lateral stripes on a silver body. It is commonly around 1 kg or just under, but can reach in excess of 2 kg. It has the typical humped Lutjanid head shape and large canine teeth. Spread along the coast from central Queensland throughout the tropics, it is a voracious, aggressive fish that will charge out and strike at lures, baits or virtually anything small enough to be edible. It is not great eating.

Fishing method

Cast small lures across shallow coral outcrops or fish strip-baits over reef areas and jiggle them, about an arm's length off the bottom. Stout mono traces are a good idea.

Pike, long-finned
Dinolestes lewini

Location/Description

The long-finned pike grows in excess of 2 kg but is common at less than 1 kg. Often confused with the smaller sea pike (*Sphyraena obtusata*), it is best distinguished by the longer length of its anal fins and its stouter body. Distributed throughout the mid to southern coastlines of Australia, it is variously described as a poor food fish, a bait-stealing pest, an entertaining light-tackle lure chaser, but most importantly, as a prime live bait for large yellowtail kingfish, mulloway and snapper.

Fishing method

Small whole fish such as whitebait, fish strips or lures, moved erratically in the manner of wounded bait fish is best. Its dagger-like teeth mean a short trace of heavier nylon is useful. Trolling from boats and also lure casting from rocks is common.

Queenfish
Scomberoides commersonianus

Also known as leatherskin, queenie, skinnyfish, skinny.

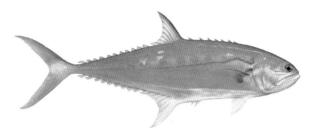

Location/Description

A fish of the tropical north, 'queenfish' is the term now coming into popular usage to describe both this fish (*S. commersonianus*) and the related *S. lysan*. A member of the trevally family, queenfish school and attack with the same ferocity as their shorter, more blunt-shaped cousins. To both the consternation and delight of anglers they often leap clear of the water in a repeated, cartwheeling motion. Queenfish, which can grow to more than 1 m long and weigh about 11 kg, move at great speed, put up a good fight when hooked, and are a fair table fish.

Fishing method

Troll the gaps between coral islands or drift over reefs and around shallow bomboras casting chrome lures or surface poppers. These fish are fun on tackle from 4 to 6 kg.

Sailfish

Istiophorus platypterus

Also known as sails.

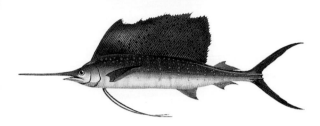

Location/Description

Found throughout Queensland and the Top End, and south as far as Exmouth in Western Australia, the sailfish is most plentiful off the Pilbara coast in the west, Moreton Bay in the east, and throughout the island complexes of the Great Barrier Reef. This most elegant of the billfish family is a prized game fish, which has in recent years become a regular target for anglers in small boats. Fish in the 20 to 40 kg bracket will gather in schools around reefs or sandy tidal bays where currents aggregate bait fish.

Fishing method

A Queensland technique is to locate a pod of midwater bait on the sounder, jig up a supply on baitfish jigs, and either rig these for trolling or present them as live baits on casting tackle to surface swimming sailfish.

Salmon, Australian

Arripis trutta

Also known as bay trout, blackback, cockie salmon, colonial salmon, kahawai, salmon trout, sambo.

Location/Description

Prized more as a fighting fish than table fare, the Australian salmon is no relation to the European salmon. It moves in schools, leaving sheltered estuary and inlet waters in its second or third year for beach, reef and ocean rock environments. The two species are the eastern salmon (*A. trutta*), which is commonly 2 to 4 kg, and a western salmon (*A. truttaceus*), which can easily top 8 kg. Adult salmon are silvery with an olive-grey back, while juvenile salmon have brown markings on their backs and sides.

Fishing method

Favourite baits are beach and bloodworms, pilchards, garfish, pippis and a variety of lures and saltwater flies. The bite of a salmon can be indecisive and its mouth is soft, so sharp hooks and a careful hand are needed to avoid it tearing free.

Salmon, threadfin

Eleutheronema tetradactylum

Also known as Burnett River salmon, king salmon, putty nose, giant threadie.

Location/Description

Threadfin salmon come in a few different colours – silver, golden and blue – and the little ones (blue), from 1 to 4 kg, are found throughout north Queensland. Strongholds of the bigger, more golden and silver fish, from 4 kg to over 20 kg, are found in the remote waters of the Top End. Threadfin are as fast as barramundi, and turn and jump with even more style and grace. They like estuarine and shallow bay waters, and are not averse to feeding in conditions that you might think are too muddy. They are excellent eating.

Fishing method

Baits of live prawns and small live fish are taken with relish at creek mouths on a high but falling tide, as are various minnow-style lures. Large, bushy saltwater flies can be cast to sighted fish cruising in the shallows.

Samson fish

Seriola hippos

Also known as sambo, samson, sea kingfish.

Location/Description

The samson fish can vary considerably in shape and colour, causing much confusion. Often mistaken for a differently coloured yellowtail kingfish, the samson fish is generally stouter in build and uniformly bronze to grey-green across the back. Common in Western Australia, it inhabits the coastal waters of Australia's east and west coasts. It is found over reefs and in water to 50 m in depth, and can top 40 kg. This large powerful game fish fights savagely when hooked; it is an excellent table fish, particularly when juvenile.

Fishing method

Bottom fish with large, live or strip baits of squid or fish, or cast, jig or troll lures. Lines can be from 6 to 8 kg but should more likely be 10 to 15, with 24-kg line. Samson fish respond to berley.

Sergeant baker

Aulopus purpurissatus

Also known as sarge.

Location/Description

Plentiful on both deep and inshore coastal reefs throughout much of the lower two-thirds of the continent, the sergeant baker commonly sits perched tripod-like on its fins, on boulders, reef bottoms or in crevices. It can be caught from boats or ocean rocks and in some exceptionally deep and clean harbours, such as Jervis Bay in New South Wales. This fish apparently takes its common name from a sergeant with the First Fleet, who reportedly first spotted it. They are a reasonable table fish.

Fishing method

Use fish baits, and allow the bait to settle where rock bottom turns to sand. Also put lures close to the bottom, where this fish spends most of its time.

Shark, bronze whaler

Carcharinus brachyurus

Also known as cocktail shark, copper shark, whaler.

Location/Description

One of many 'whaler' sharks, the bronze whaler is perhaps the best known, by reputation if not personal encounter. A potentially dangerous shark to swimmers, it is inquisitive, aggressive and when excited, quite fearless. Found with related species almost all around Australia, it roams between offshore reefs, surf beaches, estuaries and bays, and along the ocean rocks. It can be targeted by land-based gamefishers from piers and rocks. It is happy to switch from being a hunter to a scavenger as the need arises.

Fishing method

Use large, live or dead, whole-fish baits, or large slabs of cut bait, squid, fish heads etc. suspended under a balloon for a float. Large forged game-hooks and traces of 7 to 49-strand cable wire are usually employed.

Shark, gummy
Mustelus antarcticus

Also known as gummies.

Location/Description

A popular and excellent eating species, the gummy shark is often targeted by beach and boat anglers fishing at night. It grows to 1.75 m and 25 kg and is readily recognised by its uniform grey or grey-brown colour with small white spots along its back. It feeds on various bottom species including shellfish, octopus, and fish. Juvenile gummy sharks around 30–40 cm long are often caught in bays by anglers targeting snapper, flathead and other species.

Fishing method

Gummy sharks have enjoyed a population resurgence that has resulted in heightened angler interest. Most are caught in bays over snapper ground, or at night from surf beaches. Use a running sinker or running paternoster rig and 4/0 to 6/0 hooks. Best baits include pilchards, fish strips, and squid. Can be caught in shallow water at night.

Shark, mako
Isurus oxyrinchus

Also known as shortfin mako, blue pointer.

Location/Description

While it can be a nuisance to anglers fishing for tuna and billfish in northern waters, the mako is welcomed by southern anglers where those game species are rare. Reaching 4 m, its extreme aggression and tendency to leap clear of the water combined with its good eating qualities make it a popular offshore game species in the cooler ocean waters. Another pelagic shark, the blue shark or blue whaler, *Prionace glauca*, is similar in size, appearance, and distribution and is popular among southern offshore game fishers.

Fishing method

Makos are aggressive and fast and respond well to a berley trail. Large sharks are caught trolling lures and baits, or on large fish-baits suspended under a float in a berley trail. Small mako sharks have become a popular fly rod species in southern New South Wales, Tasmania and Victoria.

Shark, school
Galeorhinus galeus

Also known as greyboy, grey shark, snapper shark, tope.

Location/Description

Together with the gummy shark (*Mustelus antarcticus*), pencil shark (*Hypogaleus hyugaensis*) and whiskery shark (*Furgaleus macki*), the school shark does not attack swimmers. Unlike the gummy shark, however, it has small sharp teeth that can inflict a painful bite to a careless angler's hand. It is found offshore and within enclosed waters from Brisbane, throughout New South Wales, Victoria and Tasmania, to South Australia and just north of Perth in Western Australia. It is a small species of around 2 m in length and can attain a weight of up to 30 kg.

Fishing method

Most often trawled or long-lined by professionals, this shark will take fish-flesh baits in estuaries or over shallow reefs. It is a common catch along far eastern Victorian beaches and estuaries.

Shark, thresher
Alopias vulpinus

Also known as longtail or thintail thresher, fox shark.

Location/Description

The thresher shark is a pelagic sub-tropical and temperate water species. It is more common in oceanic and coastal waters of southern Australia, where it is targeted by game fishers. Although it grows to over 5 m, its exceptionally long tail makes up at least half its length. It has a small mouth and teeth and uses its deep cylindrical body to drive its tail to herd and stun its small prey. A careless angler can receive a severe blow, concussion and abrasions from its tail.

Fishing method

Most thresher sharks are caught accidentally on small baits by anglers fishing inshore reefs for other species such as snapper. At times appearing shy and reclusive, the thresher takes small unweighted cube baits better than the larger baits normally associated with shark fishing.

Shark, wobbegong

Orectolobus maculatus

Also known as carpet shark.

Location/Description

An exceptionally well-camouflaged species, the wobbegong lies among rocks and kelp on shallow reefs down to 100 m around southern Australia. Apart from its distinctive mottled skin pattern and tasselled snout, its other notable characteristic is its tenacious grip once it locks its jaws around its prey, bait, or a careless angler. Growing to 3.2 m and 75 kg, it is considered good eating. The banded wobbegong (*O. ornatus*) is more widely distributed in tropical and temperate waters, also occurring on shallow reefs.

Fishing method

An incidental catch by anglers bottom-fishing inshore reefs. Wobbegongs rarely take live bait but will take large fish fillets fished on the bottom. Anglers fishing from rocks often encounter them just under the surface near rock ledges and suspend a bait under a float in midwater to catch them.

Snapper
Pagrus auratus

Also known as cockney bream, red bream, reddies, schnapper, squire (juvenile).

Location/Description

The snapper is widely distributed from central Queensland, throughout New South Wales, Victoria and the two gulf regions of South Australia, into Western Australia as far north as Shark Bay. Inhabiting inshore to moderate-depth reefs, snapper is also found in major estuaries and bays. The juveniles inhabit bays and estuaries as nurseries, but the adult fish will enter large bays such as Port Phillip in Victoria. The biggest snapper in excess of 15 kg are found in the gulf waters of South Australia and Shark Bay, Western Australia.

Fishing method

Fresh baits of whole or cut fish or squid, or live baits such as yellowtail scad, slimy mackerel and garfish, are best. Use needle sharp hooks from 2/0 to 6/0, line of 4 to 8 kg, and a running sinker rig with a minimum weight. Berley helps.

Snapper, black
Lethrinus olivaceus

Also known as grass emperor, blue-lined emperor,
long-nosed emperor, small-tooth emperor.

Location/Description

Widespread across the tropical Indian
and Central Pacific Ocean region, this is
a rapid-swimming member of the
emperor family, inhabiting coral and
rocky reefs, from the shallows to depths
of 180 m. It is readily distinguished from other emperor
species by its uniform greyish colour and long snout.
Growing to 1 m and 14 kg, it is commonly caught at
sizes of around 60 cm.

Fishing method

Fish over reefs on the bottom. Use strip baits or squid and
berley, and have the bait on or suspended just off the bottom
on a paternoster rig. Hook size from No. 2 to 6/0 will suffice.
Best method is to drift and allow enough lead for the current.

Snapper, golden
Lutjanus johni

Also known as large-scale sea perch, fingermark bream, red bream.

Location/Description

Its large size combined with its excellent fighting and eating qualities makes this a popular angling fish in tropical waters. The golden snapper is readily distinguished from other tropical snappers by its rather uniform metallic, pale yellow to silvery colouring. It is common on inshore and offshore reefs and occasionally enters estuaries. It is often caught by anglers fishing around mangroves, rocky outcrops and headlands. It grows to 90 cm and is rated as an excellent table fish.

Fishing method

Heavy handlines or barra tackle is the way to go. Squid, pilchards and fish strips work well on reefs. In estuaries this fish can also be caught on lures used for barramundi. Hooks vary to suit bait. Offshore 4/0 to 6/0 would be preferred. Inshore No. 2 to 4/0 size hooks are more common.

Snapper, queen
Nemadactylus valenciennesi

Also known as southern blue morwong.

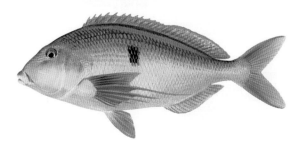

Location/Description

Anglers fishing for snapper in deeper coastal waters off Victoria to southern Western Australia occasionally take this species. It is a particularly handsome fish, blue in colour with yellow lined markings most noticeably on the head. A bottom-dwelling fish, it lives at depths of 40–240 m. Reaching lengths of 90 cm and weights of up to 12 kg, it is an excellent eating fish making these occasional catches a welcome surprise.

Fishing method

Bottom fishing on the drift over reefs is popular. Use a paternoster rig, 6/0 hooks, and bait up with craytail, squid, fish strips or pilchards.

Snapper, saddletail

Lutjanus malabaricus

Also known as redfish, large-mouth nannygai,
ruby emperor.

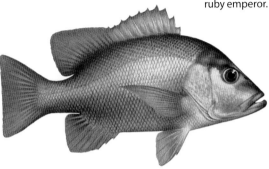

Location/Description

Adults of this handsome deep red fish
grow to 14 kg and form schools around
deeper reefs and on open bottom down
to 100 m. Juveniles are commonly
found over muddy bottom in shallower
waters. Popular among anglers in northern Australian
waters, this excellent sport fish is commonly caught at
sizes of 1–2 kg and is highly regarded as a table fish. It
often occurs in schools with the crimson sea perch
(*L. erythropterus*).

Fishing method

Bottom fish on the drift over inshore and offshore reefs. Hand
lining is a popular method. Use a paternoster rig, hooks from
4/0 to 6/0, and use fresh baits including squid, pilchards and
fish strips.

Snook
Sphyraena novaehollandiae

Also known as pike, short-finned seapike.

Location/Description

This member of the pike family inhabits cool southern waters from around Port Stephens, New South Wales, southward around the coast to Island Point in Western Australia. Favouring shallow waters to 20 m with sand to weed bottoms, the snook preys upon small bait fish, juvenile squid and various crustaceans. It is often found in the same places over periods of weeks or even years, in season. Fish average under 1 kg, but can reach over 2 kg. It is a very popular angling species in South Australia.

Fishing method

Small fish-strip baits or even lures are taken, it being best to 'jig' the offering. A trace of heavier line can help. Use bluebait or whitebait presented on linked No.1 to 2/0 hooks.

Sweep

Scorpis aequipinnis

Also known as sea sweep.

Location/Description

Juvenile sweep inhabit the New South Wales coastal estuaries and get close inshore on the rocks where they are regarded as a nuisance. Larger specimens are found over reefs. In Victoria and South Australia sweep can grow in excess of 2 kg. These fish are good table fare and on some parts of the coast, highly sought after by anglers. Sweep seem to favour the tip of breaking water near the edge of bomboras and the like. However, drifting in a boat close to the white water of breaking reefs can make serious sweep fishing a dangerous proposition.

Fishing method

Regular sweep anglers berley over shallow reefs. Small hooks, baited with peeled prawn, squid or fish flesh, are drifted down on lightly weighted rigs.

Sweetlip, grass

Lethrinus laticaudis

Also known as brown sweetlip, snapper bream, grass emperor.

Location/Description

The grass sweetlip is a strong, handsome fish of exceptional table value. Its distribution ranges from temperate to tropical waters, favouring rocky or coral reefs according to latitudes. The species is also apt to follow warm coastal currents in summer from its usual tropical haunts, as far south as central New South Wales. Common in sizes from 2 to 3 kg, grass sweetlip may surpass 6 kg, but such fish are rare these days as fishing pressure mounts on tropical coral reefs.

Fishing method

Present fresh bait close to, but just off, the bottom. Use leadhead jigs, tipped with baits of squid or fish strip, to get the bait down past the swarming lesser fry. This rig, however, must be worked or jigged up and down.

Sweetlip, red-throated

Lethrinus miniatus

Also known as red-throated emperor, sweetlip,
sweetlips emperor, tricky snapper.

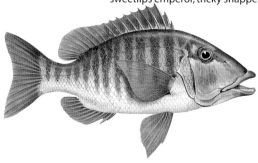

Location/Description

The attractive, powerful, red-throated
sweetlip is one of the most common of
the Lethrinidae family of emperors and
sweetlips. It ranges from temperate to
tropical waters, favouring rocky or coral
reefs according to latitudes, and is apt to follow warm
coastal currents south from its usual tropical haunts
to central New South Wales. Common in sizes from
1 to 2 kg, red-throated sweetlip rarely surpass 4 kg. It
provides excellent eating but it has been associated
with ciguatera – in north-eastern regions only.

Fishing method

Fresh bait presented just off the bottom is best. Leadhead jigs
tipped with squid or fish-strip baits can be used to ensure the
bait is not taken by other fish on the way down. If using this rig,
it must be jigged up and down.

Tailor

Pomatomus saltatrix

Also known as chopper (juvenile), pomba, skipjack.

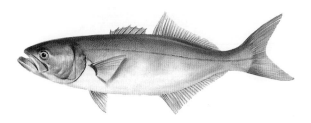

Location/Description

A saltwater favourite found throughout New South Wales, southern Queensland and the Western Australian coast south of Shark Bay, the tailor seldom attains more than 4 kg. Fish of 9 or 10 kg create a sensation when caught. Tailor frequent surf beaches, rocky headlands, offshore islands and wash areas, and can often be seen tearing up the surface under a canopy of screeching sea birds. The Fraser Island tailor run is the best known in Australia.

Fishing method

Troll tidelines and the edges of ocean rock washes, and also cast with lures or whole fish baits on ganged-hook rigs, usually comprised of three, four or even five hooks from 2/0 to 5/0 in size.

Tarwhine
Rhabdosargus sarba

Also known as silver bream.

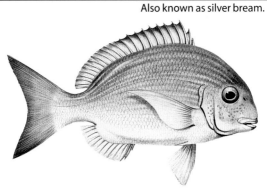

Location/Description

This member of the same family as bream and snapper has a smaller, slightly undershot mouth and a pattern of golden, wavy, horizontal lines on a silver background, which distinguish it from the similar looking yellowfin bream. Tarwhine is distributed throughout shallow reef, surf line and estuary environments, from southern Queensland, throughout New South Wales, Victoria, part of South Australia and southern Western Australia. Fish over 2 kg are occasionally caught, but half to 1 kg is the average size.

Fishing method

Baits of marine worms, prawns, nippers or shrimp are effective, particularly at coastal lake entrances during a prawn run. Tarwhine also inhabit the surf and will take baits of pippi. Hooks need to be slightly smaller than for an equivalent-sized bream.

Teraglin
Atractoscion aequidens

Also known as trag, teraglin-jew.

Location/Description

The southern teraglin is similar in appearance to the juvenile mulloway, but where the mulloway's tail is convex, the teraglin's is concave. It is commonly found from just south of Fraser Island in Queensland to Bermagui in New South Wales, and over reefy bottom in depths of something around 60 m. This species, which can grow to about 1 m and weigh about 10 kg, is related to the silver teraglin (*Otolithes argenteus*) found in more tropical waters and sometimes called 'wiretooth' or 'yankee whiting'. Both species are top-rate table fish.

Fishing method

Use baits of fish strip mounted on two linked 5/0 hooks on a short trace below a running sinker. This rig is night-fished over suitable reef area – full moon is best. Handlines around 15 to 20 kg are necessary as a lost fish can put the school off the bite.

Tommy ruff

Arripis georgianus

Also known as Australian herring, ruff, tommy rough.

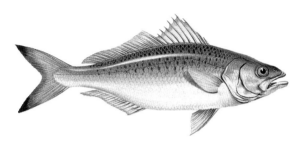

Location/Description

A member of the same family as the Australian salmon, the tommy ruff (so-called because of the rough feel of its scales) is a fish that rarely tops 40 cm in length and 800 g in weight. It is distributed widely through southern Western Australia and across South Australia. Often confused with juvenile Australian salmon, it can be distinguished by its larger eyes and black-tipped tail. The tommy ruff is fished along beaches, in estuaries and from rocky groynes, often schooling in vast numbers and hitting baits or small lures voraciously.

Fishing method

Small hooks, size 4 to 8, baited with fish flesh, prawns, or specially bred bait maggots are best. Rigs commonly incorporate some form of berley dispenser, into which an oily mix of bread, pollard fish flesh and tuna oil is pressed.

Trevalla, blue-eye
Hyperoglyphe antarctica

Also known as blue-eye.

Location/Description

Seldom caught at depths less than 100 m, the blue-eye is prevalent near drop-offs at depths of 400–600 m. Aided by modern boating and fishing technology, anglers have increasingly entered this domain, attracted by such large (up to 35 kg) fish of outstanding eating qualities. While it grows up to 1.4 m and 50 kg in weight, most of those taken are less than 10 kg. It is hard to believe that a fish that feeds largely on gelatinous plankton can grow so big and taste so good.

Fishing method

Use a gunnel-mounted winch and plenty of lead weight to get your bait down through currents to the depths. Use a paternoster rig with multiple leaders and 6/0 hooks. Blue-eye trevalla will take most fresh fish strips and squid.

Trevally, giant
Caranx ignobilis

Also known as lowly trevally, turrum.

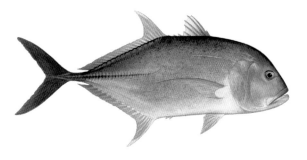

Location/Description

This fish is a strong opponent on any line class and is a slab of raw swimming power weighing in excess of 30 kg. A surface hit from one of these fish is awesome and the run is often unstoppable. The giant trevally is distributed throughout the tropics and is occasionally found in more southern waters on the east and west coasts during summer, as it follows the warm currents. It prefers rocky corners of reefs, partially submerged bomboras or the narrow tide-race passages between tropical islands and coral formations.

Fishing method

Baits of dead or live fish, or whole squid, or a variety of lures, especially surface poppers, are best. Troll or cast these and retrieve them quickly over or past preferred habitat. Giant trevally sometimes band up in packs and savage schools of smaller fish.

Trevally, golden

Gnathanodon speciosus

Also known as golden.

Location/Description

Golden trevally is a tropical species and one of the most attractive in the family. It is found in the warmer coastal waters of northern Australia and along the coast of Western Australia. Its colours are often silvery, but on capture this fish's flanks turn a more distinctive rich gold, with greenish hues across the back. A distinctive dark stripe runs down through the eye. Common from 5 to 8 kg, this fish grows in excess of 30 kg and more than 1 m long. It is a powerful, stubborn fighter and excellent table fare.

Fishing method

This trevally will take baits of fish flesh, crustaceans and small live fish, but is much better sport if pursued on lures, either jigged, trolled or cast. It will sometimes attack with such ferocity that a carelessly held rod can be torn from the angler's grasp.

Trevally, silver

Pseudocaranx dentex

Also known as blurter, croaker, silver, skipjack trevally, skippy, white trevally.

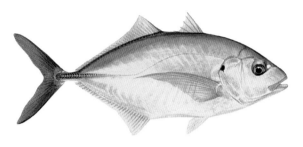

Location/Description

By far the most common trevally in cooler southern waters, this fish is normally caught in sizes ranging from half a kilogram in estuaries (juveniles), to 3 to 5 kg around reefs and open headlands (adults). The silver trevally is distributed from southern Queensland through New South Wales and into Victoria, extending southward to Tasmania and westward through South Australia into Western Australia, as far north as North West Cape. It is renowned as an excellent table fish.

Fishing method

Use strip baits of fish or squid, whole peeled prawns or small chrome lures. The fish often school offshore over reefs in 5 to 40 m of water. Depending on local conditions, you can anchor or drift over them, drop baits or lures, and expect to capture fish up to 5 kg.

Trout, coral
Plectropomus maculatus

Also known as coastal trout, island coral trout,
leopard cod trout.

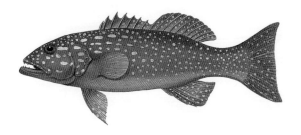

Location/Description

The coral trout is one of the most
prized sport and table fish of the north.
It inhabits both inshore and outer reefs,
the larger fish being found on the most
seaward extremities or most remote
locations. It is stout, with an amazing range of
colouration, the most common of which is a bright
red body carrying electric blue spots that become
larger and more scattered towards the head. Fish
larger than 8 kg have been implicated in ciguatera
cases, when caught off the Great Barrier Reef.
Western Australia does not have ciguatera.

Fishing method

Suspend baits just off the bottom and anchor precisely.
Alternatively, large surface poppers can be cast over coral
shallows, skipping them back over the drop-off into deeper
water. When hooked, trout run like an express train.

Trumpeter, bastard

Latridopsis forsteri

Also known as silver trumpeter.

Location/Description

This species is said to have earned its common name because it is difficult to catch. It is found in the cool marine environments of the southern states, inhabiting areas from deep offshore reefs to shallow rocky inshore waters. It grows to over 65 cm and 4 kg although most of those caught are juveniles and smaller adults, which school on shallow reefs, averaging up to 1 kg. Large fish tend to occur singly and in deeper water. It is an excellent table fish.

Fishing method

Most are caught drifting over reefs. Use a paternoster rig and hooks from No. 2 to 4/0. Keep the bait bouncing off the bottom as you drift. Will take most baits including pilchards, squid and fish strips.

Trumpeter, striped

Latris lineata

Also known as Tasmanian trumpeter, stripey.

Location/Description

This handsome, olive-striped fish grows to 1.2 m and 25 kg. Renowned as an outstanding eating fish, its numbers have been reduced through hooking, netting, and trapping, from NSW to southern Tasmania where the juveniles of 1–2 kg were once common around inshore reefs. Today, it is mainly taken by anglers bottom-bounce fishing on reefs and broken ground at depths of 50–120 m, although it does occur at depths of at least 300 m.

Fishing method

Hooks from No. 2 to 3/0 on a paternoster rig are standard for this species. Will take most baits including squid, pippis and pilchards. If you are getting bites with no hook-ups, reduce hook size as they have small mouths.

Tuna, bigeye
Thunnus obesus

Also known as big-eye.

Location/Description

The big-eye is an oceanic species occurring around most of Australia. Solitary adults can be found in offshore waters often at depths of 250 m during the day. Juveniles, up to 20 kg, school in tropical coastal waters, often mixed with other tuna species. A large predator, it feeds on a wide range of fish and on squid. Anglers often locate young big-eye swimming 50–100 m under floating objects. While most caught by anglers are around 90 cm in length, it grows to 2.4 m and over 200 kg.

Fishing method

Not commonly encountered, this fish can be caught trolling large skirted or bibbed minnow lures or bridle-rigged baitfish designed to run deep or skip along the surface. It has also been caught cubing and drifting with live bait such as slimy mackerel rigged on a 6/0 to 9/0 hook and set deep.

Tuna, longtail

Thunnus tonggol

Also known as northern bluefin tuna, northern blue.

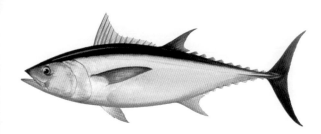

Location/Description

This species is common at 10 to 15 kg and is known to exceed 40 kg. It has a similar distribution to mackerel tuna. It is regularly taken each summer and autumn by rock anglers in New South Wales who use live bait with slimy mackerel, garfish or yellowtail scad. In Moreton Bay and various other more northerly Queensland locations, it may be spun for from boats by approaching surface-feeding schools. Of only passable food value, northern blues are essentially a sport fish or a source of bait.

Fishing method

Best methods include lure casting or live baiting from either ocean rocks, large river breakwalls, or boats. Some anglers berleying and cubing for yellowfin tuna around Bermagui have taken exceptional specimens of this fish, to 35 kg or better, on live baits.

Tuna, mackerel

Euthynnus affinis

Also known as kawakawa, mack tuna, mack, oriental bonito.

Location/Description

The mackerel tuna is a robust, tapering fish found in northern New South Wales, Queensland, Northern Territory and most of the west coast of Western Australia. It grows to a length of about 1 m and a weight of about 12 kg. A fish of both open ocean and inshore waters, it often schools with Spanish and spotted mackerel. In spring, schools of this fish gather inshore to harass glass bait fish and may enter large bays. However, these incursions are not as common as they once were, due perhaps to natural cycles of abundance and scarcity, or overfishing.

Fishing method

Lure casting with metal lures such as those that imitate small bait fish is successful from boats or ocean rocks. Also, fishing small live fish under a bobby cork is useful when they are not evident. Trolling is not a preferred option.

Tuna, southern bluefin

Thunnus maccoyii

Also known as southern blue.

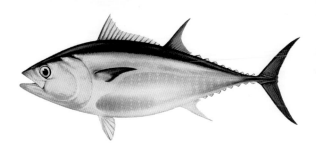

Location/Description

A more rotund and stocky tuna, the southern bluefin is one of the largest marine game fish in southern Australia. It grows to about 2 m in length and about 150 kg in weight. It was once a profitable and rich fishing resource of Australia's southern oceans, but overfishing and poor resource management led to the collapse of stocks. It is found in coastal offshore waters throughout southern Australia. An acceptable barbecue fish, the main use of southern bluefin is for canned tuna.

Fishing method

Lures, live baits and strip baits are best. It is normally taken by trolling small feather jigs at a fairly fast speed. At times it is best to lure cast from a boat. Taking from shore is rare.

Tuna, striped
Katsuwonis pelamis

Also known as skipjack tuna, stripey.

Location/Description

Striped tuna grow to about 80 cm in length and 15 kg in weight. They are found usually in large schools all around Australia, particularly in coastal waters of southern Australia. Commonly trolled from the 100-m line off coastlines from Queensland through New South Wales to Tasmania, this species is a vital link in the food chain between small ocean species and the larger game fish. Although well regarded as a sport fish, it is of poor food value unless steamed commercially, and is most often killed for bait or berley.

Fishing method

Spinning or trolling with lures from a boat is best, but it can be taken from the rocks with long casts. Lines can be down to 3 or 4 kg, but reels must have good drags and carry enough line to exhaust this determined and powerful little battler.

Tuna, yellowfin
Thunnus albacares

Also known as 'fin, Allison tuna.

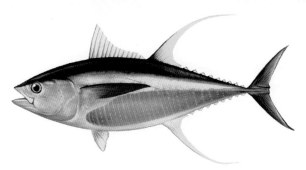

Location/Description

An important commercial species, which in angling terms has come to mean 'a threatened resource', yellowfin tuna has been targeted more in the last twenty years than in the previous hundred, probably because of the aggravated decline of southern bluefin. Found all around Australia, yellowfin comes within reach of coastal anglers most often in late summer and early autumn, when fish can vary between 15 to 50 kg. Known to grow in excess of 100 kg, this is a magnificent food and sport fish.

Fishing method

Best methods include trolling lures or live fish, such as striped tuna and frigate mackerel, or skipping dead rigged garfish. Cubing from a boat is very successful.

Tuskfish, blue
Choerodon cyanodus

Location/Description

This tropical fish occurs on shallow coastal and inshore reefs and on smooth bottom across northern Australia. It is particularly common on shallow coral reefs where it occurs in resident groups, feeding mainly on molluscs. Being a territorial fish that takes baits readily, it is prone to localised depletion in the face of heavy fishing pressure. An excellent table fish, it is commonly caught at 1–2 kg although it grows to 60 cm and 7 kg.

Fishing method

This bottom fish is caught mainly on bait such as squid and fish strips, but is sometimes caught on lures and flies. Paternoster rig works well with hooks from No. 4 to 1/0. Use light tackle to get the best sport out of this fish.

Tuskfish, Venus

Choerodon venustus

Also known as bluebone tuskfish, Venus parrotfish.

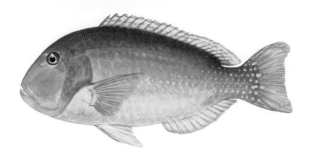

Location/Description

The Venus tuskfish is a member of the wrasse family and not hard to recognise due to its bright colouring of purples, silver and pinks. This fish is found along the east coast, north of Sydney, and across the top half of Australia. Its size varies from 2 to 5 kg, with larger specimens reaching 7 to 8 kg. Another species (C. *rubescens*), found in Western Australia between Coral Bay and Geographe Bay, grows to over 10 kg. Both species are superb fish to eat.

Fishing method

Baits of crab and cut fish are best, with double extra-strong hooks and lines. Rod and reel anglers might get by with 15 to 25-kg line on the smaller fish, which average around 5 to 6 kg, but the big adults can require heavy handlines.

Wahoo
Acanthocybium solandri

Also known as Doctor Hoo, 'hoo.

Location/Description

A tropical species of fish, loosely related to the mackerels, wahoo is found around coral reef areas of northern New South Wales, Queensland and Exmouth in Western Australia. It strays as far south as Sydney and the Sir Joseph Young Banks off Nowra, when warm northerly currents create the sparkling clean, deep blue ocean water in which you would expect to see this fish. The wahoo's speed and willingness to put up a fight make it a game fish of international note. The average size is about 15 kg.

Fishing method

Rarely caught from shore, it is usually encountered when trolling lures from a boat. Lures must be rigged on wire. Be prepared in the event of an accidental strike. Wahoo earn the ire of many marlin anglers, being capable of severing a carefully rigged marlin bait.

Warehou
Seriolella brama

Also known as blue warehou, blue trevalla, snotty, haddock.

Location/Description

Small juvenile warehou associate with large jellyfish at the surface of coastal waters while the larger adults (up to 7 kg) occur mainly on the outer continental shelf and upper slope. Of greatest interest to anglers are those of up to 1 kg, which are common in shallow coastal waters of south-eastern Australia. Locally known as snotties (because of their sliminess) and haddock in Victoria, fish of 200–500 g are often taken in large numbers by anglers who line wharves and breakwaters. Warehou are best eaten fresh.

Fishing method

This fish is a favourite among Victorian anglers fishing from piers. Warehou will take a variety of baits including pippis, mussels, raw chicken, and rabbit meat. Fish under a float, use hooks from No. 8 to No. 6 long shank and suspend the bait a couple of metres off the bottom.

Whiting, golden-lined

Sillago analis

Also known as rough-scaled whiting.

Location/Description

Typical of the several small whiting species found in Australia's shallow coastal waters, the golden-lined whiting is a schooling fish and is often taken in large numbers by anglers in Queensland. It prefers silty bottom, is usually found in bays and estuaries, and is particularly abundant around mangroves. While it reaches 45 cm, most of those caught are around 30 cm in length. The golden-lined whiting is a good table fish having firm, white, flaky flesh when cooked.

Fishing method

Prawns and sandworms will attract this species. Use a running sinker or paternoster rig, and as light a lead as conditions allow. Hook size from No. 4 to No. 6 in long-shank style works well.

Whiting, grass

Haletta semifasciata

Also known as blue rock whiting, weedy whiting, stranger.

Location/Description

This species is often taken by anglers targeting King George whiting among shallow seagrass beds and reefs in shallow coastal waters and embayments around southern Australia. A schooling fish commonly reaching 30 cm in length, its flesh is soft and of mediocre eating quality and its bones are often blue-green in colour, which some people find quite off-putting. However, it is often taken from piers and jetties by children and adult anglers keen to keep whatever they can catch.

Fishing method

This species is sometimes in plague proportions in heavily grassed bay areas. Will take mussels, pippis, sandworms and squid. Fish for them with a paternoster rig and use small hooks, about No. 8, as they have small mouths.

Whiting, King George
Sillaginodes punctata

Also known as black whiting, South Australian whiting, spotted whiting.

Location/Description

The King George whiting, the largest and tastiest of the whiting family, is plentiful in Victoria, South Australia and southern Western Australia. It is only an occasional capture in New South Wales and Tasmania. It is native to the shallow grassy flats with sand and mud bottom, although some larger fish prefer scattered offshore reefs. It grows to an impressive 60 cm or more, which translates into weights in excess of 2 kg. An important commercial catch, it is an excellent table fish.

Fishing method

Baits of mussel, pippi, skinned squid and octopus tentacle, live marine worms and pink nippers are all used. Hooks need to be small, but this can mean up to No. 1 or 1/0 for the larger fish, and No. 6 to No. 4 for the average sized fish. Line need only be 3 to 4 kg.

Whiting, sand

Sillago ciliata

Also known as bluenose whiting, sandie, silver whiting, summer whiting.

Location/Description

Abundant on the east coast, the sand whiting is commonly caught by anglers. It is found from Cape York, south along the New South Wales coast and into the East Gippsland–Lakes Entrance region of Victoria. Tasmania has a few on the eastern seaboard. Common from half to three quarters of a kilo, the sand whiting can grow in excess of 1 kg and has sweet tasting, firm flesh. It is a willing, straightforward biter on most marine worm and shellfish baits, and is fun to catch.

Fishing method

Small-gape long-shank hooks from No. 6 to No. 2 are usual in estuaries; bigger beach fish will take baits on a size No. 1 if hungry enough. Good baits are bloodworms, squirt worms, beachworms, garden worms, pippis, cockles, mussels and small soldier crabs.

Whiting, trumpeter
Sillago maculata

Also known as diver whiting, spotted whiting, winter whiting.

Location/Description

This whiting species occurs on the muddy bottoms of bays and estuaries, to depths of 30 m, across northern Australia. Preferring the turbid waters of mangrove creek mouths, they use their protruding snouts to plough through soft sediments seeking the marine worms, small crustaceans and molluscs they feed on. Growing to 30 cm, it is a popular angling species because of its fighting and eating qualities, its abundance in accessible waters, and its readiness to take bait.

Fishing method

A light tackle specialty, this species will take a variety of baits including prawns, worms, mussels and squid. Use a paternoster rig and fish near drop-offs or deeper water. Can be caught on the drift or at anchor.

Whiting, yellowfin

Sillago schomburgkii

Also known as western sand whiting.

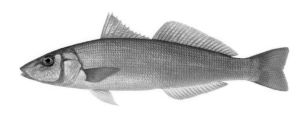

Location/Description

This schooling species is very popular among shore and boat anglers in South Australia and, particularly, in Western Australia. It occurs in large schools in shallow coastal waters and estuaries, sometimes entering brackish waters. It feeds mainly on small worms and shellfish on shallow sand flats at high tide and returns to deeper sandy areas, to 10 m depth, with the falling tide. It grows to about 40 cm in length.

Fishing method

This fish is caught using the same methods as for King George whiting. Baits include pippis, mussels, squid and sandworms. Hook size up to 1/0 but more commonly long shank from No. 6 to 4. Use a running sinker in shallow water and paternoster rig in deeper water.

Wrasse, blue-throat

Notolabrus tetricus

Also known as bluehead, bluenose parrotfish.

Location/Description

This is one of the most common fish on shallow reefs and weed beds off southern Australia. While many anglers consider the flesh soft and bland, it is in such high demand in Asian restaurants that strict controls have been imposed on recreational and commercial fishing in some states. The species has interesting behaviour when a large, dominant, brightly coloured male is removed from a school. A large female takes on the male colouration and role within weeks, changing to a male. This fish grows to 60 cm and 4 kg.

Fishing method

Most blue-throat are caught on the drift near heavy reef grounds, often alongside kelp forests. Will take most bait including fish strips, pilchards and pippis. Use hooks from size 2/0 to 4/0 on a paternoster rig. Drift for them with the bait suspended just off the bottom.

Wrasse, crimson-banded

Pseudolabrus gymnogenis

Also known as white spotted parrotfish.

Location/Description

This commonly encountered fish is one of several species known as parrotfish, so-called because of their front teeth, which form parrot-like shears. A related species, the rosy wrasse (*P. psittaculus*), is fairly common in reef areas of coastal Victoria and Tasmania. The white-spotted parrotfish commonly attains weights of 1 kg, but may be caught at several times that size. It is found on reefs from 2 m to 30 m in depth, and can dominate rock fishing captures. It is a fair table fish.

Fishing method

Use strips of fish flesh, presented near or on the bottom. It is best targeted in shallow water by dropping baits close to natural rock walls and using minimum weight to enable the bait to sink slowly.

Wrasse, Maori

Cheilinus undulatus

Also known as humphead Maori wrasse, Napoleon wrasse, giant wrasse, humphead parrotfish and double-headed wrasse.

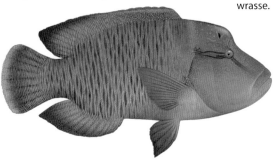

Location/Description

This is an exceptional reef species, growing to almost 2.3 m and 200 kg. It is a widespread tropical coral reef species, usually occurring singly or in pairs and feedings on shellfish at depths of 2–60 m. In Western Australia it occurs only around offshore reefs, with large territorial adults mainly occupying the deeper outer reef edges and gutters. Maori wrasse mature first as females then change to males as they grow older.

Fishing method

Fishing method is the same as for many reef species. Large hooks of about size 6/0 to 8/0 are common. Use a heavy handline and keep the bait on or suspended close to the bottom on a paternoster rig. Maori wrasse will take fish strips and squid.

Yellowtail

Trachurus novaezelandiae

Also known as yakka, yellowtail horse mackerel or yellowtail scad.

Location/Description

The yellowtail is a small pelagic fish which forms large schools in open coastal waters. While it may reach 45 cm and 1 kg, most of those frequenting inshore waters are around 20–30 cm. Keen anglers usually catch it for use as live bait for larger pelagic fish, but it also gives children and occasional anglers a great deal of fun when fishing from piers and breakwaters. Like others in the trevally family, yellowtail frequently have a large tongue-biter louse inside their mouths.

Fishing method

Sought mainly for bait, yellowtails are attracted to a fine-mist berley. Many anglers employ baitfish jigs, others simply berley heavily, bring these fish to the surface in a feeding frenzy and offer them unweighted bait, usually of small fish pieces. Use hooks from No. 6 to 8.

Freshwater Fish

Bass, Australian
Macquaria novemaculata

Also known as bass, perch.

Location/Description

This native freshwater fish hits lures and baits with an aggression out of proportion to its size, and it fights hard when hooked. Bass to 4 kg have been caught in impoundments, but a 2 kg fish is regarded as big in its natural environment – that is, southern and eastern coastal freshwater and estuarine river systems. Bass favour snaggy corners and bank sides strewn with logs, reeds and boulders, and require brackish water to spawn in late winter.

Fishing method

Anglers now fish for bass with lures instead of baits. Lures work just as well, are more fun to fish with, and suit catch-and-release fishing. Trolling and lure casting work well in both rivers and impoundments. As a sport fish, bass is usually released on capture.

Blackfish, freshwater

Gadopsis marmoratus

Also known as slippery, marble cod.

Location/Description

Blackfish have a scattered distribution in the Murray-Darling system and coastal streams of the south-east and Tasmania, preferring cool slow-flowing tributaries. Anglers targeting river blackfish often fish at night, taking advantage of the species's mainly-nocturnal feeding habits, and seek out small clear streams containing logs and other complex structure, plus dense fringing vegetation. In the more inaccessible parts of some southern coastal streams, blackfish of 3–5 kg can be found, but most of those caught are in the range of 200–450 g.

Fishing method

Blackfish are caught near logs and snags. Most anglers use a float rig and employ scrubworms and crickets for bait. Use hooks from No. 6 to 8. After dark can be a productive time to fish, and a light stick on the float will keep you in touch with events.

Carp, European
Cyprinus carpio

Also known as common carp.

This fish is extremely widespread, from the sub-tropics to the alpine regions of Victoria, New South Wales and, recently, Tasmania. Of the various imported species of fish introduced into Australian waters, carp is considered the greatest pest. It can grow to a length of 1.2 m and can weigh in excess of 15 kg. It is neither a good table fish nor a good sport fish, and it threatens the habitat of many native species. Its feeding techniques stir up silt, which reduces the oxygen output of native aquatic plants and smothers the eggs of trout and native fish.

Fishing method

Carp respond to berleying and fishing with baits of maggots, sweet corn, dough, bardi grubs or scrubworms. Fisheries regulations in enlightened States require that once caught, carp should never be put back.

Catfish, eel-tailed

Tandanus tandanus

Also known as dewfish, freshwater catfish, kenaru,
freshwater jewfish.

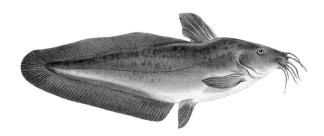

Location/Description

Eel-tailed catfish occur in various forms; the *Tandanus* species is found throughout the inland and coastal freshwater of much of south and eastern Australia. It has thrived in many water supply impoundments. This species is usually mottled grey to russet brown and averages 1 to 2 kg. Like many catfish, the dorsal and pectoral spines can inflict nasty wounds. It needs careful handling when brought in. Despite its appearance, the catfish is considered by some to be a prize table fish, once the skin has been peeled away.

Fishing method

Catfish is not generally caught on lure or fly. It is more usually targeted with baits of peeled crayfish tail, a bunch of worms or bardi grub. Fish these baits on light line with a running sinker rig over a shelving soft bottom, especially at night.

Cod, Mary River
Maccullochella peelii mariensis

Also known as greenfish.

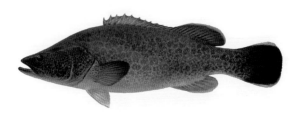

Location/Description

While it is a critically endangered species and fully protected in most of its natural range, the Mary River cod may be taken in a dozen or so artificial impoundments in Queensland, where it has been stocked for recreational fishing. It reaches sizes of up to 20 kg, but most of those caught are much smaller. Like the closely related Murray cod, the smaller legal-sized Mary River cod are good eating; however, most anglers choose to release them.

Fishing method

This fish is mainly caught on lures trolled or spun. Like its close relative the Murray cod, this species is a predator and will lie in ambush in snags for its prey. Tactics are the same as for Murray cod.

Cod, Murray
Maccullochella peelii peelii

Also known as goodoo, Murray, codfish.

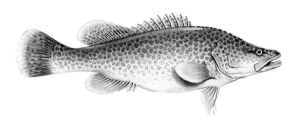

Location/Description

Attaining a length of about 1.8 m and a weight of up to 115 kg, the Murray cod is the largest and most famous native freshwater table fish. It is actually found well beyond the confines of the Murray River, being distributed throughout the Murray–Darling Basin and also stocked in many popular impoundments. Related species include the protected trout cod, the Clarence River cod, the Mary River cod and the protected eastern cod. Those caught usually average from 6 to 8 kg.

Fishing method

Cod will take lures, flies and baits. Tackle should be 4 to 10 kg depending on the terrain; in the Murray River, where the fish are big, 15 kg is not too heavy. They can be taken by trolling or casting lures, or bottom fishing or 'bobbing' baits of bardi grub, worms or crayfish.

Cod, sleepy
Oxyeleotris lineolatus

Location/Description

Anglers often take sleepy cod along with species like Australian bass, golden perch, barramundi, saratoga and tarpon in still or slow-moving waters in impoundments, streams and billabongs. It prefers snags and weed beds. The sleepy cod has been stocked in a number of Queensland impoundments for recreational fishing. However, despite its rating as an excellent table fish, its poor fighting qualities and readiness to take baits intended for more desirable species have resulted in it being regarded as a nuisance. It grows to 50 cm and over 2 kg.

Fishing method

Use a running sinker rig, baited with a local food like yabbie or shrimp. Use a hook size from No. 6 to 4. Light tackle from 3–4 kg will get the most out of this slow fish. It is a good, fun fish for beginners.

Eel, short-finned

Anguilla australis

Also known as freshwater eel, silver eel.

Location/Description

A freshwater species that migrates to salt water to spawn, the short-finned eel is common in dams, swamps, rivers and estuaries throughout much of eastern Australia, including Tasmania, and extending offshore to Lord Howe and Norfolk islands and New Zealand. Olive-green to brown in colour, it grows in excess of 6 kg and over 1 m in length. This eel will eat almost anything that presents itself, whether alive or dead, but is essentially carnivorous.

Fishing method

Baitfishing with fish strips, worms or bardi grubs is best. Hooks can be 1/0 to 2/0, rigged with a small running sinker. Use 4 to 6-kg line or risk having the line broken by the eel's vigorous struggles, particularly when it is about to be landed.

Grunter, sooty
Hephaestus fuliginosus

Also known as black bream, sooties.

Location/Description

This species generally weighs around half a kilogram but will grow in excess of 4 kg, at which size it is a formidable opponent on light tackle. The sooty grunter is but one form of the large and varied grunter family known for its pugnacious nature. It is found in both inland and coastal fresh water from near Emerald in Queensland, northwards over the Top End and south to the Kimberley region. Sooty grunters like snags, overhanging foliage, corners and deep holes.

Fishing method

Sooty grunters will attack lures as readily as baits, but are a lot more fun on artificials. Use a light threadline outfit, with 2 to 4 kg line.

Macquaria ambigua

Also known as callop, yellowbelly.

Location/Description

Naturally occurring throughout the Murray–Darling system in New South Wales, and southern Queensland, into Victoria and South Australia, the golden perch has also been artificially stocked in a number of alpine and coastal drainage impoundments. Stocky, deep-bodied fish, goldens commonly range from 1 to 3 kg in rivers and farm dams, and can reach 5 or 10 kg in major impoundments. It is a popular fish with anglers for its table quality.

Fishing method

Baits of crayfish, bardi grub and shrimp are effective, as are diving lures with the capability of 3 to 5 m depth. Casting or trolling lures around suitable stands of drowned timber is effective in impoundments. Bait fishing is more effective in turbid (muddy) rivers.

Perch, jungle
Kuhlia rupestris

Also known as junglies, rock flagtail, mountain trout.

Location/Description

A tropical freshwater native fish, the jungle perch is found in northern coastal streams, usually in estuaries, but moves freely into fresh water. It is silvery with reddish-brown markings and some black colouration on the second dorsal fin and tail fin. Its relatively slow breeding cycle, coupled with the fact that its habitat is under threat in Queensland, means its future is in jeopardy. If you can find a jungle perch at all, it will probably be half a kilo or so, much less than its once common weight of 1 to 2 kg.

Fishing method

Strictly a catch-and-release proposition. Jungle perch show a willingness to strike at lures and baits, particularly surface lures, and will take small swimming plugs as used for sooty grunter or bass. Please fish with barbless hooks.

Also known as mackas, Macquarie, mountain perch, silvereye, black bream.

Location/Description

The Macquarie perch, a shy, cryptic fish of freshwater streams, can grow to 46 cm in length and 3.5 kg in weight. Competition from introduced species and the erection of weirs and dams restricting its spawning grounds have caused a reduction in numbers. The best places to catch a Macquarie perch are Lake Dartmouth and the upper Mitta Mitta River in Victoria. While it does exist in some New South Wales rivers such as the Lachlan, Nepean and Shoalhaven, its threatened status means it is totally protected in that State.

Fishing method

A light paternoster rig with worm or mudeyes as bait is best. Also good is jigging small spoons around sunken timber, using tiny minnow lures or trout flies. The fish is usually found in between 5 to 10 m of water around trees.

Perch, silver

Bidyanus bidyanus

Also known as bidyan, black bream, silvers.

Location/Description

The natural distribution of this fish is throughout the Murray–Darling Basin, but it has been translocated to impoundments throughout southern Queensland, much of New South Wales and into Victoria, with minor stockings in parts of South Australia. Once considered the carp of the inland, silver perch, which can grow to a length of 40 cm and a weight of 8 kg, are now rare in rivers. Silver perch prefer timbered and weedy water with moderate depth and good clarity. The silver perch is an acceptable table fish, having firm, dry, white flesh.

Fishing method

Best baits are worms, grubs, crickets, grasshoppers, mudeyes and yabbies. Riverine dwellers seem to prefer small wobbling or spinning lures, but larger impoundment fish can fall for lures aimed at golden perch or Murray cod.

Redfin
Perca fluviatilis

Also known as English perch, reddies, redfin perch.

Location/Description

The redfin, an introduced species, has a propensity to overbreed and produce what is called a 'stunt' fishery of voracious tiddlers. If kept in check by predators, the redfin can grow to a respectable 3 kg and is quite good food and fair sport too. Its track record of taking over to the detriment of native species means it should never be stocked or returned to the water once caught. This fish has now infiltrated most of the eastern States' fresh water, petering out in the warmer waters of Queensland.

Fishing method

Any freshwater bait, such as worms, crickets, mudeyes, yabbies or bardi grubs, is best. They will take almost any small lure or fly, particularly small metal fish-shaped lures, jigged in deep water over schools located by an echo sounder.

Salmon, Atlantic
Salmo salar

Location/Description

Land-locked populations of Atlantic salmon are maintained by stocking in Burrinjuck Dam and Lake Jindabyne, in New South Wales, where they are fished for along with trout. Renowned overseas for its excellent fighting and eating qualities, it has not lived up to its reputation in these lakes, yielding poor returns of mainly immature fish of less than 1 kg. More recently, an exciting development in Tasmania has seen the establishment of outstanding fishing for Atlantic salmon of 3–5 kg that escape from sea-farming cages on the south-east and west coasts.

Fishing method

Bait fishing, trolling, spinning and fly fishing methods have all been used for this species. Small bladed lures have proven successful when spinning, with bibbed minnows and winged lures best for trolling. Bait includes scrubworms, minnow and glassies fished under a float. Flies such as the Tom Jones, BMS and Mrs Simpson are good.

Salmon, Chinook
Oncorhynchus tshawytscha

Also known as quinnat salmon.

Location/Description

This salmon has established a well-earned reputation in several stocked western Victorian lakes, particularly Lake Purrumbete. Few reach four years of age, but while most of those caught in recent years have weighed less than 3 kg, fish of up to 11 kg have been recorded from this lake. Along with brown trout and rainbow trout, it thrives on the plentiful galaxids, gudgeons and other small fish and invertebrates. It is keenly sought for its fighting and eating qualities.

Fishing method

Mudeye, worm or glassie fished under a bubble float is the most common method used for this species. Trolling, using downriggers to keep the lure deep, also works well. They respond to a berley trail and have been caught on pilchard strips with this technique. Fly fishers prefer flies such as the BMS, Tom Jones and gold beadhead nymphs.

Saratoga, eastern
Scleropages leichardti

Also known as Dawson River barramundi,
spotted barramundi, toga.

Location/Description

This smaller of the two saratogas,
averaging 1 to 3 kg, is distributed
throughout central Queensland fresh
water from about Fairbairn Dam, near
Emerald, up to the tip of Cape York.
This species favours pandanus-lined creeks and
billabongs, but has adapted to warm water storages
with reed and rush-bed edges. Only smaller saratoga
are suitable for the table as the large fish tend to be
flavourless and coarsely textured. Anglers should treat
them as a catch-and-release species as they are a very
long-living fish.

Fishing method

Troll or cast swimming minnows, bladed lures or surface
poppers. In tight-pocket water pinpoint presentation works
best. Lines of 4 to 6 kg are ideal, and traces of heavier nylon,
roughly twice the mainline thickness, are suitable.

Also known as toga, northern spotted barramundi.

Location/Description

Distributed across the Top End through Arnhem Land, but petering out west and south of Darwin, the gulf saratoga also extends into the western drainage areas of lower Cape York. It is usually caught around 3 to 4 kg, with exceptional fish reaching 6 to 7 kg. It can be distinguished from the eastern saratoga which has red crescent-shaped markings on its scales. Saratoga fishing is edge fishing: the edges of riverbanks, billabong cut-backs, drowned stands of paperbarks and pandanus forests.

Fishing method

Casting with lures and flies is effective. Work poppers at dawn and dusk or in shady areas, and toss sinking lures such as rattling spots and soft plastics into lily patches.

Trout, brook

Salvelinus fontinalis

Also known as brookies, brook char.

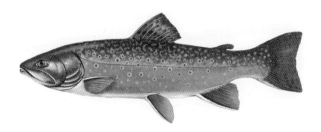

Location/Description

Brook trout, actually a form of North American char, were first introduced in the 1870s, but have not acclimatised with the same success as browns and rainbows. Their distribution is patchy in most alpine regions of Australia, notably within Lake Jindabyne, and some streams within the New England area of New South Wales. One of the most important populations exists in Tasmania's Clarence Lagoon. Common sizes are between half a kilo and 2 kg.

Fishing method

Flies, bait or lures can be used. In lakes, they respond to fly fishing from the bank perhaps more readily than to other methods, and opinion is divided whether bait fishing or fly fishing is better in streams.

Trout, brown
Salmo trutta

Also known as brownie, brown, German trout, Englishman.

Location/Description

The brown trout originated in Europe and has been successfully introduced into New South Wales and Victoria, with Tasmania having perhaps some of the best 'wild' brown trout fishing in the world. Nearly all alpine regions capable of sustaining trout have been stocked with browns, most notably Lake Eucumbene in New South Wales, which has a successful spawning run into the Eucumbene River most winters. Browns are commonly caught from half a kilo up to 2 kg, but can exceed 5 kg in some waters.

Fishing method

The best methods are wet or dry fly fishing, spinning with small-bladed lures, or using Glo-bugs and trailing nymph rigs on fish that gather in pre-spawning aggregations. Browns also readily take baits of worms, yabbies, mudeyes, live crickets and grasshoppers.

Trout, rainbow
Oncorhynchus mykiss

Also known as bows, rainbows, sea-run trout, steelhead.

Location/Description

This flashy, attractively coloured fish needs artificial stocking to maintain numbers. This is due to the fact that it spawns after the brown trout and the results are less productive. Distributed widely throughout Tasmania, Victoria and alpine regions of New South Wales, the rainbow seems to prefer faster, rocky streams, and deeper, colder lakes. It is also found in certain areas of South Australia and Western Australia. This fish commonly attains 1 to 2 kg, but is capable of growing to 6 kg or more.

Fishing method

Best methods are bait fishing or alternatively trolling and spinning for most small to average fish, and fly fishing for the large specimens. Trolling very early in the morning is preferred once the warmer weather arrives.

Index

bows (rainbow trout, rainbows, sea-run trout, steelhead) (*Oncorhynchus mykiss*) 178

bream, black (southern black bream, southern bream) (*Acanthopagrus butcheri*) 36

bream, pikey (black bream) (*Acanthopagrus berda*) 37

bream, yellowfin (eastern black bream, sea bream, silver bream, surf bream) (*Acanthopagrus australis*) 38

broad-barred Spanish mackerel (grey mackerel, greys, broad-bars) (*Scomberomorus semifasciatus*) 80

brook trout (brookies, brook char) (*Salvelinus fontinalis*) 176

brown sweetlip (grass sweetlip, snapper bream, grass emperor) (*Lethrinus laticaudis*) 124

brown trout (brownie, German trout, Englishman) (*Salmo trutta*) 177

brown-spotted rock cod (estuary cod, greasy cod, north-west groper) (*Epinephelus coioides*) 43

buffalo bream (silver drummer) (*Kyphosus sydneyanus*) 50

bully mullet (sea mullet, hardgut mullet, poddy mullet, grey mullet) (*Mugil cephalus*) 96

Burnett River salmon (threadfin salmon, king salmon, putty nose, giant threadie) (*Eleutheronema tetradactylum*) 108

butterfish (mulloway, jew, jewie, jewfish, river kingfish, soapie) (*Argyrosomus hololepidotus*) 98

callop (golden perch, yellowbelly) (*Macquaria ambigua*) 167

carp, European (common carp) (*Cyprinus carpio*) 160

carpet shark (wobbegong shark) (*Orectolobus maculatus*) 116

catfish (cobbler, estuary catfish) (*Cnidoglanis macrocephalus*) 40

catfish, eel-tailed (dewfish, freshwater catfish, kenaru, freshwater jewfish) (*Tandanus tandanus*) 161

catfish, forktailed (croaker, salmon catfish) (*Arius leptaspis*) 39

channel rat (sand flathead (southern), bay flathead, sandy) (*Platycephalus bassensis*) 56

chopper (tailor, pomba, skipjack) (*Pomatomus saltatrix*) 126

coastal trout (coral trout, island coral trout, leopard cod trout) (*Plectropomus maculatus*) 134

cobbler (catfish, estuary catfish) (*Cnidoglanis macrocephalus*) 40

cobia (black king, black kingfish, cobe, crab-eater, ling, sergeant fish) (*Rachycentron canadus*) 41

cockie salmon (Australian salmon (bay trout, blackback, colonial salmon, kahawai, salmon trout, sambo) (*Arripis trutta*) 107

cockney bream (snapper, red bream, reddies, schnapper, squire) (*Pagrus auratus*) 117

cocktail shark (bronze whaler shark, copper shark, whaler) (*Carcharinus brachyurus*) 111

cod, barramundi (humpback cod) (*Cromileptes altivelis*) 42

cod, estuary (brown-spotted rock cod, greasy cod, north-west groper) (*Epinephelus coioides*) 43

cod, Mary River (greenfish) (*Maccullochella peelii mariensis*) 162

cod, Murray (goodoo, Murray, codfish) (*Maccullochella peeli peeli*) 163

cod, Rankin (Rankins rock cod) (*Epinephelus multinotatus*) 44

cod, red (bearded rock cod) (*Pseudophycis bachus*) 45

cod, reef (estuarine rock cod, greasy cod, groper) (*Epinephelus tauvina*) 46

cod, sleepy (*Oxyeleotris lineolatus*) 164

colonial salmon (Australian salmon, bay trout, blackback, cockie salmon, kahawai, salmon trout, sambo) (*Arripis trutta*) 107

common carp (European carp) (*Cyprinus carpio*) 160

common mackerel (slimy mackerel, blue mackerel, slimies) (*Scomber australasicus*) 83

copper shark (bronze whaler shark, cocktail shark, whaler) (*Carcharinus brachyurus*) 111

Cox's hairtail (hairtail, Australian hairtail, largerhead hairtail) (*Trichiurus lepturus*) 64

crab-eater (cobia, black king, black kingfish, cobe, ling, sergeant fish) (*Rachycentron canadus*) 41

creek red bream (mangrove jack, dog bream, red bream, jack, mangrove snapper, rock barramundi) (*Lutjanus argentimaculatus*) 68

croaker (black jewfish, spotted croaker, spotted jewfish) (*Protonibea diacanthus*) 70

croaker (fork-tailed catfish, salmon catfish) (*Arius leptaspis*) 39

croaker (silver trevally, blurter, silver, skipjack trevally, skippy, white trevally) (*Pseudocaranx dentex*) 133 darkie (luderick, blackfish, nigger) (*Girella tricuspidata*) 79

dart, swallowtail (billy lids, dart, surf trevally) (*Trachinotus coppingeri*) 47

Dawson river barramundi (eastern saratoga, spotted barramundi, toga) (*Scleropages leichardti*) 174

dewfish (eel-tailed catfish, freshwater catfish, kenaru, freshwater jewfish) (*Tandanus tandanus*) 161

dhufish (Westralian jewfish, jewie, West Australian jewfish) (*Glaucosoma hebraicum*) 72

dingo fish (barracuda, cuda) (*Sphyraena barracuda*) 31

diver whiting (trumpeter whiting, spotted whiting, winter whiting) (*Sillago maculata*) 151

Doctor Hoo (wahoo, 'hoo) (*Acanthocybium solandri*) 145

dog bream (mangrove jack, creek red bream, red bream, jack, mangrove snapper, rock barramundi) (*Lutjanus argentimaculatus*) 68

doggies (school mackerel) (*Scomberomorus queenslandicus*) 81

dolphin fish (dollies, dorado, Mahi Mahi) (*Coryphaena hippurus*) 48

dorado (dolphin fish, dollies, Mahi Mahi) (*Coryphaena hippurus*) 48

Dory, John (St Peter's fish, dories, johnnies) (*Zeus faber*) 49

double-headed wrasse (Maori wrasse, humphead Maori wrasse, Napoleon wrasse, giant wrasse, humphead parrotfish) (*Cheilinus undulatus*) 155

drummer, silver (buffalo bream) (*Kyphosus sydneyanus*) 50

eastern black bream (yellowfin bream, sea bream, silver bream, surf bream) (*Acanthopagrus australis*) 38

eastern pearl perch (pearl perch, pearlie, nannygai) (*Glaucosoma scapulare*) 102

eel, short-finned (freshwater eel, silver eel) (*Anguilla australis*) 165

elephant fish (elephant shark) (*Callorhinchus milii*) 51

emperor, red (emperor, government bream) (*Lutjanus sebae*) 52

emperor, spangled (iodine bream, yellow sweetlip, north-west snapper) (*Lethrinus nebulosus*) 53

English perch (redfin, reddies, redfin perch) (*Perca fluviatilis*) 171

Englishman (brown trout, brownie, German trout) (*Salmo trutta*) 177

estuarine rock cod (reef cod, greasy cod, groper) (*Epinephelus tauvina*) 46

estuary catfish (cobbler, catfish) (*Cnidoglanis macrocephalus*) 40

fingermark bream (golden snapper, large-scale sea perch, red bream) (*Lutjanus johni*) 119

flagtail flathead (sand (northern) flathead) (*Platycephalus arenarius*) 55

flathead, dusky (black flathead, flatty, lizard) (*Platycephalus fuscus*) 54

flathead, sand (northern) (flagtail flathead) (*Platycephalus arenarius*) 55

flathead, sand (southern) (bay flathead, sandy, channel rat) (*Platycephalus bassensis*) 56

flathead, southern blue-spot (yank flathead, long nose, sandies, shovel nose) (*Platycephalus speculator*) 57

flathead, toothy (yellowfinned flathead) (*Neoplatycephalus aurimaculatus*) 58

flounder, small-toothed (*Pseudorhombus jenysii*) 59

flying gurnard (red gurnard) (*Chelidonichthys kumu*) 63

fox shark (thresher shark, longtail thresher, thintail thresher) (*Alopias vulpinus*) 115

freshwater catfish (eel-tailed catfish, dewfish, kenaru, freshwater jewfish) (*Tandanus tandanus*) 161

freshwater eel (short-finned eel, silver eel) (*Anguilla australis*) 165

freshwater jewfish (eel-tailed catfish, dewfish, freshwater catfish, kenaru) (*Tandanus tandanus*) 161

freshwater perch (estuary perch, Australian perch, perch) (*Macquaria colonorum*) 100

'gai (nannygai, goat, nanny, redfish) (*Centroberyx affinis*) 99

garfish, eastern sea (garie, beakie, red beak) (*Hyporhamphus australis*) 60

German trout (brown trout, brownie, Englishman) (*Salmo trutta*) 177

giant herring (milkfish, Moreton Bay salmon) (*Chanos chanos*) 89

giant perch (barramundi, barra) (*Lates calcarifer*) 32

giant threadies (threadfin salmon, Burnett River salmon, king salmon, putty nose) (*Eleutheronema tetradactylum*) 108

giant wrasse (Maori wrasse, humphead Maori wrasse, Napoleon wrasse, humphead parrotfish, double-headed wrasse) (*Cheilinus undulatus*) 155

goatfish (red mullet) (*Upeneichthys vlamingii*) 94

golden trevally (golden) (*Gnathanodon speciosus*) 132

goodoo (Murray cod, Murray, codfish) (*Maccullochella peeli peeli*) 163

government bream (red emperor, emperor) (*Lutjanus sebae*) 52

grass emperor (black snapper, blue-lined emperor, long-nosed emperor, small-tooth emperor) (*Lethrinus olivaceus*) 118

grass emperor (grass sweetlip, brown sweetlip, snapper bream) (*Lethrinus laticaudis*) 124

greasy cod (estuary cod, brown-spotted rock cod, north-west groper) (*Epinephelus coioides*) 43

greasy cod (reef cod, estuarine rock cod, groper) (*Epinephelus tauvina*) 46

greenfish (Mary River cod) (*Maccullochella peelii mariensis*) 162

grey mackerel (broad-barred Spanish mackerel, greys, broad-bars) (*Scomberomorus semifasciatus*) 80

grey morwong (blue morwong, mowie) (*Nemadactylus douglasii*) 91

grey mullet (sea mullet, bully mullet, hardgut mullet, poddy mullet) (*Mugil cephalus*) 96

grey shark (school shark, greyboy, snapper shark, tope) (*Galeorhinus galeus*) 114

groper (reef cod, estuarine rock cod, greasy cod) (*Epinephelus tauvina*) 46

groper, baldchin (Venus tuskfish, blue parrot) (*Choerodon rubescens*) 61

groper, blue (bluey) (*Achoerodus viridis*) 62

grunter, sooty (black bream, sooties) (*Hephaestus fuliginosus*) 166

gummy shark (gummies) (*Mustelus antarcticus*) 112

gurnard, red (flying gurnard) (*Chelidonichthys kumu*) 63

haddock (warehou, blue warehou, blue trevalla, snotty) (*Seriolella brama*) 146

hairtail (Australian hairtail, Cox's hairtail, largerhead hairtail) (*Trichiurus lepturus*) 64

hapuku (New Zealand groper, hapuka) (*Polyprion oxygeneios*) 65

hardgut mullet (sea mullet, bully mullet, poddy mullet, grey mullet) (*Mugil cephalus*) 96

herring, oxeye (tarpon) (*Megalops cyprinoides*) 66

'hoo (wahoo, Doctor Hoo) (*Acanthocybium solandri*) 145

hoodlum (yellowtail kingfish, bandit, king) (*Seriola lalandi*) 74

hornpike long tom (slender long tom, needlefish) (*Strongylura leiura*) 78

horse mackerel (bonito, bonnie, horsie) (*Sarda australis*) 35

humpback cod (barramundi cod) (*Cromileptes altivelis*) 42

humphead parrotfish (Maori wrasse, humphead Maori wrasse, Napoleon wrasse, giant wrasse, double-headed wrasse) (*Cheilinus undulatus*) 155

hussar (*Lutjanus adetii*) 67

Indo-Pacific blue marlin (blue marlin, blues) (*Makaira nigricans*) 87

iodine bream (spangled emperor, yellow sweetlip, north-west snapper) (*Lethrinus nebulosus*) 53

island coral trout (coral trout, coastal trout, leopard cod trout) (*Plectropomus maculatus*) 134

jack, mangrove (creek red bream, dog bream, red bream, jack, mangrove snapper, rock barramundi) (*Lutjanus argentimaculatus*) 68

jackass fish (jackass morwong, perch, terakihi) (*Nemadactylus macropterus*) 92

jackets (toothbrush leatherjacket, pale brown leatherjacket) (*Acanthaluteres vittiger*) 76

Japanese mackerel (spotted mackerel, snook, spottie, Australian spotted mackerel) (*Scomberomorus munroi*) 85

javelin fish (barred grunter, trumpeter, spotted grunter, spotted javelin fish) (*Pomadasys kaakan*) 69

jewfish (mulloway, butterfish, jew, jewie, river kingfish, soapie) (*Argyrosomus hololepidotus*) 98

jewfish, black (spotted croaker, spotted jewfish, croaker) (*Protonibea diacanthus*) 70

jewfish, little (silver jewfish) (*Johnius vogleri*) 71

jewfish, Westralian (dhufish, jewie, West Australian jewfish) (*Glaucosoma hebraicum*) 72

Job-fish, rosy (king snapper, rosy snapper) (*Pristipomoides filamentosus*) 73

John Dory (St Peter's fish, dories, johnnies) (*Zeus faber*) 49

jungle perch (junglies, rock flagtail, mountain trout) (*Kuhlia rupestris*) 168

kahawai (Australian salmon, bay trout, blackback, cockie salmon, colonial salmon, salmon trout, sambo) (*Arripis trutta*) 107 kawakawa (mackerel tuna, mack tuna, mack, oriental bonito) (*Euthynnus affinis*) 139

kenaru (eel-tailed catfish, dewfish, freshwater catfish, freshwater jewfish) (*Tandanus tandanus*) 161

King George whiting (black whiting, South Australian whiting, spotted whiting) (*Sillaginodes punctata*) 149

king salmon (threadfin salmon, Burnett River salmon, putty nose, giant threadie) (*Eleutheronema tetradactylum*) 108

king snapper (rosy Job-fish, rosy snapper) (*Pristipomoides filamentosus*) 73

kingfish, yellowtail (bandit, hoodlum, king) (*Seriola lalandi*) 74

ladyfish (bonefish) (*Albula vulpes*) 34

lano (sand mullet, sandie, tallegalane) (*Myxus elongatus*) 95

large-mouth nannygai (saddletail snapper, redfish, ruby emperor) (*Lutjanus malabaricus*) 121

largerhead hairtail (hairtail, Australian hairtail, Cox's hairtail) (*Trichiurus lepturus*) 64

large-scale sea perch (golden snapper, fingermark bream, red bream) (*Lutjanus johni*) 119

large-scaled tuna (shark mackerel, scaly mackerel, sharkie) (*Grammatorcynus bicarinatus*) 82

leatherjacket, six-spine (*Meuschenia freycineti*) 75

leatherjacket, toothbrush (jackets, pale brown leatherjacket) (*Acanthaluteres vittiger*) 76

leatherskin (queenfish, queenie, skinnyfish, skinny) (*Scomberoides commersonianus*) 105

leopard cod trout (coral trout, coastal trout, island coral trout) (*Plectropomus maculatus*) 134

ling (cobia, black king, black kingfish, cobe, crab-eater, sergeant fish) (*Rachycentron canadus*) 41

ling, rock (ling) (*Genypterus tigerinus*) 77

lizard (dusky flathead, black flathead, flatty) (*Platycephalus fuscus*) 54

long nose (southern blue-spot flathead, yank flathead, sandies, shovel nose) (*Platycephalus speculator*) 57

long tom, slender (hornpike long tom, needlefish) (*Strongylura leiura*) 78

longfin tuna (albacore) (*Thunnus alalunga*) 28

long-nosed emperor (black snapper, grass emperor, blue-lined emperor, small-tooth emperor) (*Lethrinus olivaceus*) 118

longtail thresher (thresher shark, thintail thresher, fox shark) (*Alopias vulpinus*) 115

lowly trevally (giant trevally, turrum) (*Caranx ignobilis*) 131

luderick (blackfish, darkie, nigger) (*Girella tricuspidata*) 79

mackas (Macquarie perch, Macquarie, mountain perch, silvereye, black bream) (*Macquaria australasica*) 169

mackerel tuna (kawakawa, mack tuna, mack, oriental bonito) (*Euthynnus affinis*) 139

mackerel, grey (broad-barred Spanish mackerel, greys, broad-bars) (*Scomberomorus semifasciatus*) 80

mackerel, school (doggies) (*Scomberomorus queenslandicus*) 81

mackerel, shark (large-scaled tuna, scaly mackerel, sharkie) (*Grammatorcynus bicarinatus*) 82

mackerel, slimy (blue mackerel, common mackerel, slimies) (*Scomber australasicus*) 83

mackerel, Spanish (narrow-barred mackerel, narrow-barred Spanish mackerel, Spaniards, Spanish) (*Scomberomorus commerson*) 84

mackerel, spotted (Japanese mackerel, snook, spottie, Australian spotted mackerel) (*Scomberomorus munroi*) 85

Macquarie perch (mackas, Macquarie, mountain perch, silvereye, black bream) (*Macquaria australasica*) 169

Mahi Mahi (dolphin fish, dollies, dorado) (*Coryphaena hippurus*) 48

mangrove snapper (mangrove jack, creek red bream, dog bream, red bream, jack, rock barramundi) (*Lutjanus argentimaculatus*) 68

marble cod (freshwater blackfish, slippery) (*Gadopsis marmoratus*) 159

marlin, black (black, silver marlin, silver) (*Makaira indica*) 86

marlin, blue (blues, Indo-Pacific blue marlin) (*Makaira nigricans*) 87

milkfish (giant herring, Moreton Bay salmon) (*Chanos chanos*) 89

moonfish (moony, short-finned batfish) (*Zabidius novemaculeatus*) 90

Moreton Bay salmon (milkfish, giant herring) (*Chanos chanos*) 89

morwong, blue (grey morwong, mowie) (*Nemadactylus douglasii*) 91 morwong, jackass (perch, jackass fish, terakihi) (*Nemadactylus macropterus*) 92

morwong, red (sea carp) (*Cheilodactylus fuscus*) 93

Moses snapper (Moses perch, Moses sea perch, black-spot sea perch) (*Lutjanus russelli*) 101

mountain perch (Macquarie perch, mackas, Macquarie, silvereye, black bream) (*Macquaria australasica*) 169

mountain trout (jungle perch, junglies, rock flagtail) (*Kuhlia rupestris*) 168

mowie (blue morwong, grey morwong) (*Nemadactylus douglasii*) 91

mullet, red (goatfish) (*Upeneichthys vlamingii*) 94

mullet, sand (lano, sandie, tallegalane) (*Myxus elongatus*) 95

mullet, sea (bully mullet, hardgut mullet, poddy mullet, grey mullet) (*Mugil cephalus*) 96

mullet, yelloweye (pilch) (*Aldrichetta forsteri*) 97

mulloway (butterfish, jew, jewie, jewfish, river kingfish, soapie) (*Argyrosomus hololepidotus*) 98

Murray cod (goodoo, Murray, codfish) (*Maccullochella peeli peeli*) 163

nannygai ('gai, goat, nanny, redfish) (*Centroberyx affinis*) 99

nannygai (pearl perch, eastern pearl perch, pearlie) (*Glaucosoma scapulare*) 102

nanny-goat (nannygai, 'gai, goat, redfish) (*Centroberyx affinis*) 99

Napoleon wrasse (Maori wrasse, humphead Maori wrasse, giant wrasse, humphead parrotfish, double-headed wrasse) (*Cheilinus undulatus*) 155

narrow-barred mackerel (Spanish mackerel, narrow-barred Spanish mackerel, Spaniards, Spanish) (*Scomberomorus commerson*) 84

needlefish (slender long tom, hornpike long tom) (*Strongylura leiura*) 78

New Zealand groper (hapuku, hapaka) (*Polyprion oxygeneios*) 65

nigger (luderick, blackfish, darkie) (*Girella tricuspidata*) 79

northern bluefin tuna (longtail tuna, northern blue) (*Thunnus tonggol*) 138

northern spotted barramundi (gulf saratoga, toga) (*Scleropages jardini*) 175

north-west groper (estuary cod, brown-spotted rock cod, greasy cod) (*Epinephelus coioides*) 43

north-west snapper (spangled emperor, iodine bream, yellow sweetlip) (*Lethrinus nebulosus*) 53

oriental bonito (mackerel tuna, kawakawa, mack tuna, mack) (*Euthynnus affinis*) 139

pale brown leatherjacket (toothbrush leatherjacket, jackets) (*Acanthaluteres vittiger*) 76

perch (Australian bass, bass) (*Macquaria novemaculata*) 158

perch (jackass morwong, jackass fish, terakihi) (*Nemadactylus macropterus*) 92

perch, estuary (Australian perch, freshwater perch, perch) (*Macquaria colonorum*) 100

perch, golden (callop, yellowbelly) (*Macquaria ambigua*) 167

perch, jungle (junglies, rock flagtail, mountain trout) (*Kuhlia rupestris*) 168

perch, Macquarie (mackas, Macquarie, mountain perch, silvereye, black bream) (*Macquaria australasica*) 169

perch, Moses (Moses sea perch, Moses snapper, black-spot sea perch) (*Lutjanus russelli*) 101

perch, pearl (eastern pearl perch, pearlie, nannygai) (*Glaucosoma scapulare*) 102

perch, silver (bidyan, black bream, silvers) (*Bidyanus bidyanus*) 170

perch, stripey sea (stripey snapper, stripey) (*Lutjanus carponotatus*) 103

pickhandle (barracouta, axehandle, couta) (*Thyrsites atun*) 30

pig (rock blackfish, black drummer, blackfish) (*Girella elevata*) 33

pike (snook, short-finned seapike) (*Sphyraena novaehollandiae*) 122

pike, long-finned (*Dinolestes lewini*) 104

pilch (yelloweye mullet) (*Aldrichetta forsteri*) 97

poddy mullet (sea mullet, bully mullet, hardgut mullet, grey mullet) (*Mugil cephalus*) 96

pomba (tailor, chopper, skipjack) (*Pomatomus saltatrix*) 126

putty nose (threadfin salmon, Burnett River salmon, king salmon, giant threadie) (*Eleutheronema tetradactylum*) 108 queenfish (leatherskin, queenie, skinnyfish, skinny) (*Scomberoides commersonianus*) 105

quinnat salmon (chinook salmon) (*Oncorhynchus tshawytscha*) 173

rainbow trout (bows, rainbows, sea-run trout, steelhead) (*Oncorhynchus mykiss*) 178

Rankins rock cod (Rankin cod) (*Epinephelus multinotatus*) 44

red beak (eastern sea garfish, garie, beakie) (*Hyporhamphus australis*) 60

red bream (golden snapper, large-scale sea perch, fingermark bream) (*Lutjanus johni*) 119

red bream (snapper, cockney bream, reddies, schnapper, squire) (*Pagrus auratus*) 117

redfin (English perch, reddies, redfin perch) (*Perca fluviatilis*) 171

redfish (nannygai, 'gai, goat, nanny) (*Centroberyx affinis*) 99

redfish (saddletail snapper, large-mouth nannygai, ruby emperor) (*Lutjanus malabaricus*) 121

red-throated emperor (red-throated sweetlip, sweetlip, sweetlips emperor, tricky snapper) (*Lethrinus miniatus*) 125

river kingfish (mulloway, butterfish, jew, jewie, jewfish, soapie) (*Argyrosomus hololepidotus*) 98

rock barramundi (mangrove jack, creek red bream, dog bream, red bream, jack, mangrove snapper) (*Lutjanus argentimaculatus*) 68

rock flagtail (jungle perch, junglies, mountain trout) (*Kuhlia rupestris*) 168

rock ling (ling) (*Genypterus tigerinus*) 77

rosy snapper (rosy Job-fish, king snapper) (*Pristipomoides filamentosus*) 73

rough-scaled whiting (golden-lined whiting) (*Sillago analis*) 147

ruby emperor (saddletail snapper, redfish, large-mouth nannygai) (*Lutjanus malabaricus*) 121

ruff (tommy ruff, Australian herring, tommy rough) (*Arripis georgianus*) 129

sailfish (sails) (*Istiophorus platypterus*) 106

salmon catfish (forktailed catfish, croaker) (*Arius leptaspis*) 39

salmon trout (Australian salmon, bay trout, blackback, cockie salmon, colonial salmon, kahawai, sambo) (*Arripis trutta*) 107

salmon, Atlantic (*Salmo salar*) 172

salmon, Australian (bay trout, blackback, cockie salmon, colonial salmon, kahawai, salmon trout, sambo) (*Arripis trutta*) 107

salmon, Chinook (quinnat salmon) (*Oncorhynchus tshawytscha*) 173

salmon, threadfin (Burnett River salmon, king salmon, nasty nose, giant threadie) (*Eleutheronema tetradactylum*) 108

sambo (Australian salmon, bay trout, blackback, cockie salmon, colonial salmon, kahawai, salmon trout (*Arripis trutta*) 107

samson fish (sambo, samson, sea kingfish) (*Seriola hippos*) 109

sand flathead (southern) (bay flathead, sandy, channel rat) (*Platycephalus bassensis*) 56

sand mullet (lano, sandie, tallegalane) (*Myxus elongatus*) 95

sand whiting (bluenose whiting, sandie, silver whiting, summer whiting) (*Sillago ciliata*) 150

sandies (southern blue-spot flathead, yank flathead, long nose, shovel nose) (*Platycephalus speculator*) 57

saratoga, eastern (Dawson River barramundi, spotted barramundi, toga) (*Scleropages leichardti*) 174

saratoga, gulf (toga, northern spotted barramundi) (*Scleropages jardini*) 175

sarge (sergeant baker) (*Aulopus purpurissatus*) 110

scaly mackerel (shark mackerel, large-scaled tuna, sharkie) (*Grammatorcynus bicarinatus*) 82

schnapper (snapper, cockney bream, red bream, reddies, squire) (*Pagrus auratus*) 117

sea bream (yellowfin bream, eastern black bream, silver bream, surf bream) (*Acanthopagrus australis*) 38

sea carp (red morwong) (*Cheilodactylus fuscus*) 93

sea kingfish (samson fish, sambo, samson) (*Seriola hippos*) 109

sea sweep (sweep) (*Scorpis aequipinnis*) 123

sea-run trout (rainbow trout, bows, rainbows, steelhead) (*Oncorhynchus mykiss*) 178

sergeant baker (sarge) (*Aulopus purpurissatus*) 110

sergeant fish (cobia, black king, black kingfish, cobe, crab-eater, ling) (*Rachycentron canadus*) 41

shark mackerel (large-scaled tuna, scaly mackerel, sharkie) (*Grammatorcynus bicarinatus*) 82